W9-AGZ-427

Perseverance
Missions to the WORLD

BARBARA PLAUGHER

To Colleen
a fellow LION
& friend

Barbara Plaugher

© 2016 Barbara Plaugher
All rights reserved. No part of this publication may be reproduced, stored in a retrieval system or transmitted, in any form, or by any means, electronic, mechanical, photocopying, recording, or otherwise, without the prior permission of the publishers.

For information or additional copies contact:
Barbara Plaugher
62 Anna Circle
Bluffton, OH 45817

Carlisle Printing
OF WALNUT CREEK LTD
800.927.4196 · carlisleprinting.com
Sugarcreek, Ohio 44681

This book is dedicated to my four children...
Roger, Randall, Susan and Mary.

PERSEVERANCE

*The humorous and adventurous experiences of a Nurse
desiring to serve others.*

Table of Contents

Foreword

This book is written to share with those who have a desire to serve others in a most rewarding way. As a nurse in a service occupation, this passion for volunteering has developed more over time, and my only regret is that I didn't begin earlier with my volunteer service, and now I have run out of my most productive years in my life, making some volunteer efforts difficult. Perhaps after reading about my experiences, my thoughts, the humor and fulfillment that I have experienced, others may find the inspiration to follow and step out into the world of service for others, whether in their chosen occupation or by service to others through volunteering.

I do want to emphasize that there is always a need that can be met, whether locally, throughout our country or in third-world countries around the world. With the many organizations seeking volunteers and the many people needing assistance, one would have no problem in choosing a way to serve others. I chose to volunteer with medical service, as will be shared later on in this book.

Many people have asked about what is the reward for volunteer work? Unless you have tried it, perhaps you cannot understand the most fulfillments you experience is in helping others. It is that smile, hug, or thank you that you receive, that carries you on with enthusiasm.

How does one decide to serve others? Does the drive come from genetics or from what we experience in our lives? Or both? I now can look back over the past many years and see how this desire has developed and materialized.

II.   My father was a generous man, helping others throughout his life that ended at age 74 with a rapidly spreading cancer. My mother was a private individual. I like to think that I am more like my father. Growing up was helping my father around the farm. Climbing in the barn was such a delight to me as a child. Living on a farm was a great way to learn responsibility with caring for the animals and all the other tasks that it entails.

Throughout my childhood I was a happy child, except when falling through a hole in the haymow into the pig pen below and thus breaking my arm. This ended in my being admitted to a hospital and placed into traction. This was my first experience into the medical field, other than getting rabies shots because one of our horses had a problem. That was no fun, going to the old-fashioned doctor's office for the dreaded "shots" and having to be caught and held down for the painful injections.

I was busy in our small local school with the studies and all the activities it offered. Graduation was coming soon and I needed to make a decision which way to go in my life's direction. At this time in society most girls became teachers or nurses. That was the choice.

Becoming a nurse was the best decision I could have made for a life-long commitment, even though my decision was made on selfish reasons. I was dating my husband-to-be at the time and looked at a three- year (33 month) education in a nursing school verses a four-year college education. It would be sooner to be married and start a family, I thought, as many of my friends had married soon after graduation from high school. Needless to say, I did not know at the age of 17 that I would later complete my bachelor's degree and obtain a master's degree before the age of 50, during the same years my children were in college.

In 2015 I was recognized for 50 years of service in our local hospital and then decided to "hang up my hat" from the hospital at the age of 78½ years; however, my plans were to continue serving the underserved wherever I could.

III.   My nursing history took me to employment in physician's offices and local hospitals, part-time in both facilities during the same time period. I loved the variety that I found in a small community hospital. I am copying a narrative written for my 35 year service awards program booklet in 2001…

The hiring and orientation process was certainly different 35 years ago. I walked into Bluffton Community Hospital at 9 a.m., was hired, and asked to come to work at 3 p.m. that same day. I told my husband that it must have been the way I wore my hair, back in a bun as that was the Grace Kelly era, and I must have looked similar to others in this Mennonite community, because at that time I was the only "outsider" working in the hospital. All other employees were natives of Bluffton and/or the LPN nursing school that had been provided at the hospital.

Bluffton Community Hospital was a frugal hospital. Years ago the financial statements were always in the black. I learned this very quickly. During a hasty delivery of a baby, I threw away the string that tied the sterile packet together. I was gently scolded by the superintendent and told to rewrap the string back onto the ball of string kept in the surgery sterilization room.

One of our most exciting times was when our only surgeon brought his personal friend from California in for surgery. I was the 3-11 nurse who did the prep and enema on the patient, Phyllis Diller. Try to top that in your memoirs! This was my first "claim to fame", giving an enema to Phyllis Diller. And what a stir her arrival made. We set up a four-bed ward as her private suite. She and husband, Fang, made themselves comfortable, while calls from Bob Hope and others streamed into the hospital. Actually there was not a phone in her room, so as her private duty nurse, I spoke to Bob Hope on a near-by phone and relayed his message to Phyllis. Flowers filled the room sent from the "movie stars" in California. Bluffton Hospital made national news and our little hospital was on the map.

Working 3-11 and going home to bed late at times made sleeping difficult. I remember working in the emergency department when this man came in literally scalped. His scalp was hanging back onto his shoulders after his head went through the windshield of his car. After work I went home, woke up my husband and described the gruesome accident to him. I then turned over and went to sleep, as he lay in bed, wide-eyed and unable to sleep.

One thing I do want to emphasize is that in all my years of nursing I have respected the privacy of the patient's personal information. If an incident was discussed, no name was attached to it. I am so adamant that the patient's information and personal privacy belongs to the patient.

We worry about JCAHO, the official accreditation agency of the hospital, but once you have been through a HCFA, the Medicare survey agency, and the nurse surveyor asks you to explain which direction you wipe a thermometer, up or down, we soon learn to expect any ridiculous questions during these times.

I had learned x-ray skills while working for an orthopedic group and continued assisting in the radiology department and covering call for the hospital. Since the Director of Radiology also worked as the head of the laboratory, I was taught to work in the lab. That was in the era of mouth pipetting. My biggest frustration was doing a pregnancy test with the live frogs that we kept in the crisper drawer of the refrigerator. Occasionally one of those slimy critters would get out and hop around on the laboratory floor, as I was trying to catch it.

I was the Director of Nursing from 1975 until 1985 and then Director of Patient Services from 1985 until I moved my office to Blanchard Valley Hospital in 1995 and became a merged employee as both facilities joined together. At Blanchard Valley I worked closely with the medical staff in the quality assurance and improvement activities, leading the efforts in JCAHO compliance and accreditation. I worked with our lawyer for the risk management compliance and enjoyed this aspect of my job, while auditing a post-graduate health law class taught by the CEO of the hospital at the Medical College of Ohio. I have met many interesting people over the years and have had the opportunity to work in a variety of positions during that time, thus making a nursing career a wise choice and rewarding experience for me.

IV.   For the hospital's recognition banquet of 40 years, I wrote the following...

I now feel that I have made a complete circle. I graduated from high school in 1954 and immediately went to work at a Lima Bank in the proofreading department. I am now still proofreading charts for medical records, quality and utilization review. I guess it is better than a person I once interviewed, who told me that she was a "sorter". She sorted various items at every job where she had worked. Anyway back to the bank, which was my summer job before nursing school. In order to resign from the bank, I had to talk to the bank President, and he said that I would remember this job, when I was carrying bedpans.

I feel that nursing has been the best pursuit of a career that I could have made, as I have always enjoyed variety, the challenge, working with and serving people. During my three years of nursing school, I worked at Hardin Memorial in Kenton on my vacation time. I really enjoyed the small hospital, so after working one year at Lima Memorial, I came to Bluffton Hospital in 1958. Starting a family took me from the nursing service for a period of six months after my second child. After the third child was born, while still in the Bluffton Hospital as a patient, I was asked to take x-ray call from my hospital bed for one evening. I agreed and got paid 25 cents per hour for a total of $4.00. However, I was sure happy that no patient came in for an x-ray during that period of time. In 1963, $4.00 helped quite a bit towards my hospital bill. My last child, born in 1965, put me back to work at the hospital without a break in service. I continued x-ray call for 13 years prior to beepers. I would station my kids by the telephone at home after supper, while I took the table scraps out to the chicken yard, as I didn't want to miss any incoming calls.

Living on a farm to raise a family was great. It taught our children responsibility and how to work. We also had great social times. The Bluffton Hospital held their picnics at our pond. For many years Halloween parties in the haunted woods with a wiener roast and hayride provided much entertainment for up to 200 people in an evening. We were pleased when the Findlay Hospital CEO and wife attended one Halloween party and thoroughly enjoyed the event, adding that we need to charge an entrance fee for such a delightful event.

We recently met the now retired CEO at a hospital event and sat at the same table for the evening. Upon greeting us he asked if we were still having those delightful Halloween parties that he enjoyed so much. Perhaps twenty years or more have passed since our last party, but pleasant memories linger on.

V.   Excerpts from memorable events…

Over the years I worked in obstetrics and taught pre-natal classes. I loved the educational part of nursing and helping others.

I worked in the emergency department and took the first coronary class offered in this area, at Lima Memorial Hospital in 1969. After these classes I was coming to work and going to save everyone with the new CPR classes fresh in my mind. I then taught classes for preliminary coronary care, as Bluffton Hospital set up their coronary unit. We had an invasive cardiologist who insisted that we insert Swan catheters. We were honored to have the Director of Nursing from a larger hospital came to observe before starting this procedure in their hospital. I enjoyed working in surgery and caused quite a stir as second scrub nurse when the surgeon asked the assistant surgeon to "turn the tips" the other way, referring to the Curved Kelly instruments. I had just shifted my weight, and turned my body slightly from the retracting position, when the assistant surgeon indicated that he was talking to him and that the surgeon was not asking me to turn my "tips". Poor timing!! This incident was told many times and even at the surgeon's retirement party. The small hospital gave me a challenge and an opportunity to work in many areas and serve others.

Other funny incidents I remember was when drawing blood from a local doctor, he let out a yell, just as a joke. I got so frustrated that I ended up placing the blood in the wrong drawing tube and thus had to call him back for a re-stick. That was the last time he pulled his prank.

One of my most competent nurses came to me with a questionable situation when I was Director of Nursing. She was quite upset. We had a new Canadian doctor writing orders and he had written for the nurses to observe for "pussy" discharge. I explained that this referred to pus, not pussy. She was so embarrassed.

On one April fool's day I was called back to the maternity department as one of our nurses was carrying a newborn down the hall and pushing the crib. This is entirely unacceptable as babes need to be placed in their cribs during the process of removing the babe from the nursery to the mother's room; however, as soon as she saw me she stumbled and the new born "resussie baby" fell to the floor. What an April fool's joke. I nearly fainted!

My first obligation as a nurse was to prepare the patient before the doctor would arrive for treatment. A patient came into the ED department with a laceration on his scalp. I therefore cleaned and shaved a small area around the laceration, as I had been trained. When the doctor came in he informed me that his way of treating scalp lacerations was to take the hair from the area and tie it into a knot, thus pulling the laceration edges together. I knew from then on how this particular doctor treated scalp lacerations, as he never let me forget! This same doctor would treat dislocated shoulders by taking off his shoe and placing his foot in the patient's armpit to relocate the shoulder. I learned a lot by the old-fashioned treatment that I never saw in my nursing elsewhere. And actually it all worked as we continued to care for the community needs.

You learn to work with the doctors and their personalities. One physician seemed to be perplexed when I would try to anticipate his needs with the patient. Even to the fact that as he was sniffing while helping in the x-ray department, I offered him a Kleenex. Instead he decided to wipe his nose on his sleeve.

As a 3-11 supervisor in our small hospital, I was the only RN staffed. Besides the routine patient care, one evening we had three deliveries. I relied upon my experienced LPN staff for support. Most of these nurses had been trained in the hospital and were quite capable of excellent care. I loved the delivery of babies. A nice happy, healthy part in the life of a nurse. I do remember one case that was quite traumatic. I was to drop ether for anesthesia. This particular patient had a real reaction to the ether and got her leg out of the stirrups and kicked the doctor in the chest, sending him reeling back to the wall. He was not happy, to say the least! However, all turned out well for the mother and the beautiful new baby.

These individual thoughts of mine along with many that resurface at times are part of my life and love for the service industry that we call nursing. Coming to work in a 19 bed hospital with 21 patients to care for was a usual practice in the 1960's. We always expected patients lining the halls. Since that time, we now find the beds hard to fill or patients are in an out-patient status. Change has been drastic in the health care field. However, the need to serve those in need continues.

Office work was also a joy as you meet such interesting people and soon they become to trust your judgment and feel that your interest in them is sincere. The man who presented to ask the doctor to see his wife because....mama was flowing like the Mississippi River; another patient was writing his book and going off to dig for silver in Mexico and needed some financial support from the local doctor. Patients who would bring their ails to the window with either a bottle of smelly poop or needing information about their "privates" sending our secretary into shutters. This was all in the day of the medical staff. What could be more interesting than people?

VI.   Volunteer services began…

My husband and I did some volunteer work as counselors for a youth group. We also visited a store front church for the homeless one cold January evening. This was a sad day for the homeless as one of their members had frozen to death under a bridge the night before. It was an interesting concept to see these people in this store front church, as it reminded me of patients I had taken care of in the state mental institution. You could see the paranoid, the catatonic and others. The state institution had been closed, as it was felt that locking up these people was cruel and inhumane treatment, now some lived under bridges and froze to death. The more we became involved with volunteer service, the more we felt the need to serve.

I had been enjoying medical mission work on my vacation time since 1994. This has taken me to many countries. With the training and jobs that I have had as a nurse, the coordinating of these missions came quite easily and became quite rewarding. In 1997 I had the opportunity to begin the coordination of many missions that I attended, along with some that I only pulled together for another team. I had been hoping to continue in this mission work for many years to come.

In 2013 I was chosen to receive the Albert E. Dyckes Health Care Worker of the Year for the state of Ohio, presented by the Ohio Hospital Association, what an honor for myself and the hospital. Much of the criteria used to make the final choice for this award came from volunteer service. I will now share some of those experiences.

VII.   Volunteer Service

I always felt that I would like to volunteer on the Good Ship Hope and perhaps be a scrub nurse. However, by the time my children were raised the years had passed for this strenuous job. I read in the local newspaper that a local optometrist had completed an eye care mission into Central America, so I called him asking if another mission came up, would he consider asking my husband and myself to participate. Therefore in 1994 I joined with a VOSH (Volunteer Optometric Services to Humanity) team with the thought that if I didn't like it, it was only one week out of my life. As of 2015 I had completed my 20th mission.

All my mission work, except one mission to Haiti, was done with the Volunteer Optometric Services to Humanity. VOSH is an organization dedicated to providing vision care to the underserved around the world. Members of this organization include optometrists, ophthalmologists, opticians, and trained laypersons. All members pay for their own expenses and donate their services for the joy of helping others.

Dr. Franklin Harms, an optometrist in Hillsboro, Kansas started VOSH in the early 1970's. He felt compelled to do something for his fellow man. The first VOSH Kansas project was a "fly-in" mission into Mexico in 1972. Two of the volunteers were pilots; one an optometrist, one an ophthalmologist.

When the team arrived at the border of Mexico, customs agents could not believe this group would take all those glasses into Mexico and not try to sell them for a profit. (The same thing happens yet today as teams work to get through customs). For this reason the team was forced to leave one person behind and he was replaced with an armed Mexican representative.

When the plane neared the dirt landing strip at the edge of town, the strip was covered with small Mexican burros. As the two pilots radioed back and forth, it was decided that one plane would buzz the strip to try to move the burros out of the way. It was later commented, "Those burros moved so fast they likely ended up somewhere in South America". Once the Mexican officials were convinced the VOSH team was truly in the country to give vision to those-in-need, one of the pilots was allowed to go back and claim the "hostage".

This happened in 1972 and continues as of today. When a VOSH-Ohio team landed on a grass strip in Hinche, Haiti in 2010, there were others there to keep the animals out of the way for the team to land. Armed guards are usual for VOSH teams going into third-world countries. The team going into Venezuela was under the protection of the National Guard back in 2001, this happened three months prior to a coup of the President in that country.

If you like to serve your fellow man and have a little adventure in your life, VOSH is the organization that provides this opportunity. VOSH-Ohio was started in 1987 by a local optometrist, Dr. Darrell Groman. He asked a local church group in a neighboring town to begin an eye glass sorting center in order to obtain used eyeglasses for his missions.

Since that time the sorting center has grown and now takes over an older kitchen area in the basement of the United Methodist Church in Pandora, Ohio. Over 150,000 glasses come into the sorting center each year. Volunteers process these glasses in order to have clean, usable glasses for the VOSH-Ohio missions, and also for other missions if extra glasses are available.

Volunteers for missions have come from all over the States, and occasionally from different countries. There are 33 VOSH organizations worldwide. International VOSH established a website in 1999. Information on upcoming missions and past missions are available on this site. www.vosh.org

VOSH-Ohio also has a website... www.voshohio.com. This website lists upcoming missions, along with previous missions and how to become a member of VOSH-Ohio.

My First Mission
into Central America

The first mission was with VOSH, Volunteer Optometric Services to Humanity, into Santa Barbara, Honduras in 1994, a regional center that dates from the late colonial period and located in the western part of the country, where people live in extreme poverty. Our team consisted of 19 members. We were welcomed with cases of warm coke and beer by our host. My first photo taken, after arriving at the airport, was of all the people crawling into the back of pick-up trucks. What a sight to see!

We stayed overnight in San Pedro Sula in an economy hotel, to say the least. We walked to the square and had dinner at the Grand Hotel, then a late night walk back to our hotel through the surrounding area past people living on the street, fires burning as they cooked their food, and beggars with their hands out, was eye opening to me. Perhaps this wasn't the safest area to venture out.

Mariachi bands roamed the streets and we contracted with one to play some music for the team as we sat on the steps outside the hotel. This created a rival with another band and nearly caused a fight. Finally beggars drove us inside. When we were assigned to our room for the evening, the hotel employee would open the door and spray it thoroughly with foul-smelling bug spray. We wondered what all kind of varmints were inside. A bright light outside our window illuminated the room. The air conditioner was loud, the tile floor dirty, dirty painted walls; I pulled hair and other spots off the sheets. My husband was not happy! I awoke in the morning with three swollen bites on one leg. I thought this is a perfect way to start a mission with possible cellulitis! Thank goodness for antibiotic ointment.

Sunday morning we arose bright and early to walk out onto our balcony to view the city. What we saw was a man using a nearby statue of Chieftan Lempira as a urinal. We experienced for the first time a shower with an electric shower head. I was almost afraid to touch it, as you have to turn it on with the water running, and I was afraid of being shocked. So we just took cold showers and got onto the bus traveling to Santa Barbara.

We stayed in a boarding house and heard fireworks during the night, along with a few gun shots. This was over the Thanksgiving break. Many street children lived in a local church in Santa Barbara. The Peace Corps workers had taught these children to shine shoes. So when our truck would roll into town after clinic was finished, the boys would run behind the truck with their shoe shine kits and gather at the boarding house, offering their services. Most of the team would have their shoes shined, including tennis shoes. This was a more respectful way of providing money for the children

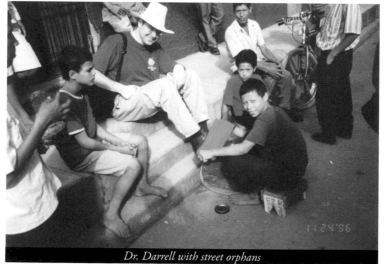

Dr. Darrell with street orphans

than handing out money to the beggars on the street. We were told that we would be eating our meals at Donna Anas, costing each team member $1.86/day for 3 meals. Such an interesting restaurant, it was almost like home with many tables and chairs in one room.

We worked with a retired Peace Corps worker, Dolores, who took handicapped children into her home and helped them to be transferred to Shriners Hospital, here in the States, for surgery and then to return back to her care. She was an interesting woman, previously from California, who volunteered for the Peace Corps at the age of 58, after her husband died. After her Peace Corps stint she remained in Santa Barbara, and worked with the Honduran children. We walked to Dolores' home and saw her children that she was keeping at the present time. Her home has four bedrooms filled with cribs and youth beds. We walked through the markets, seeing the fresh vegetables, fruit and meats hanging (along with hog heads), and met our Peace Corps workers that we would be working with during the clinics.

Monday we were up at 4 am, had our breakfast at Donna Anas, and now we were in the back of a pick-up truck at 6 am to travel to our first clinic site. I was sure to get a photo of our team in the back of the pickup, as this was a first for me. We had a two-hour trip on a dirt road, riding up through the misty clouds into the mountains, before reaching El Nispero. Clinic was to be held in a local school and patients were lined up waiting to receive their free eye care and glasses if needed. Many of our patients were illiterate and it was difficult to orient them to the acuity that I was doing at that time. Even our interpreters had difficulty. We examined 350 appreciative patients on our first day of clinic. We saw the young girls weaving mats, as they sat on the floor, in nearby houses. The trip home was in the open truck bed and we arrived back after dark accompanied by a full moon. We dropped one Peace Corp worker off to walk a dark path to her village. She is braver than I. She was a delightful girl helping others while living in a house with a mud floor and no windowpanes. Supper was red beans, rice, tacos, cheese and some kind of meat. One team member told me that the meat was probably "road kill" and soon I stayed to eating just the rice and beans. Lots of pineapple, melon and watermelon were available.

On Tuesday we again rode in the back of the pick-up truck to El Nispero and cared for 450 patients that day. All patients were so glad to be able to see clearly and be able either to read, sew, do their wood working or carry on with their daily activities much better. We were a guest of the town and were able to visit the artisans and purchase some of their hand-crafts. Our Peace Corps worker also brought some crafts from her village. Some village dignitaries played on a "wood pile", wooden xylophone, and provided such beautiful mariachi music for our team. It was great, until it broke! Again we rode back to the boarding house by moonlight, dropping off our interpreters at their own villages. We were told that there are over 200 Peace Corps workers here in Honduras. By the time we arrived at our restaurant there was no electricity and we ate by

Peace Corp workers join the team, along with a local street orphan

candlelight. We did have generator power at the hotel. Red beans and rice. I have gotten tired of the food already and I was just plain tired.

Wednesday we climbed into the truck and we were off to Concepcion del Sur with 16 members in the back of the truck and 6 up in the front. This was a shorter ride on a paved road and a nicer village. We were located in a school close to a new town hall and we visited nearby shops. Only 250 grateful patients were seen today, as one nearby village did not arrive at our clinic. Team members are beginning to get gastro-intestinal upsets. Trip back for supper with no electricity, cold showers, candles, and loud generator at the boarding house.

Our VOSH team is an interesting group. We have two diabetics and one optometrist with cancer. I have found that people with their own problems are most giving to others. These people are fun-loving non-complaining people who help others. What a joy!

Thursday we again went back to Conception del Sur. The small villages where we held clinics had animals walking in and out of the clinic grounds. We completed our clinics seeing a total of 1,500 patients. I didn't count the animals! All patients were very grateful and the kids followed the Gringos everywhere. There was a farewell ceremony by the officials of the village in the park with speeches of gratitude. Again we loaded 16 members in the back of the truck along with boxes of glasses. We were really packed in, and 6 more team members were in the front of the truck traveling to our boarding house.

We then packed in a bus and traveled from Santa Barbara to San Pedro Sula. We arrived at the Gran Sula Hotel with many boxes and luggage to the beautiful accommodations for three nights. And I got to eat good spaghetti!

Friday we took a trip to a banana plantation, mahogany wood carving shop and botanical gardens. At the mahogany wood shop in El Progresso many young boys were becoming apprentices to the business. Beautiful ornate furniture was being carved. At the unique botanical gardens, formerly the United Fruit Company experimental station, we saw large termite nests and tall bamboo. We also stopped at Tela on the beach. Tela is a banana port of clapboard houses with attractive beaches. At one time Tela was the principal port of the United Fruit Company and you could still see ships being loaded with bananas at the Tela pier. Conch shells and coconuts were for sale on the beach. The Bay Islands are close-by. These islands are inhabited by merchant seamen and skilled boat builders and fishing remains the most important occupation, although tourism was becoming fast a more significant part of the population.

On Saturday we took a trip to the amazing Copan Ruins. Copan was the Athens of the Mayan world. Here at Copan there are more carved monuments than at other ruin sites. This area may have been settled as early as 2000 B.C. We learned of the rise and fall of this civilization. We climbed on the huge boulders, viewed the various courts and experienced the kids outside of the ruins begging for coins as we entered. When we declined, they would ask our name and say "maybe later". When we came out to get on our bus, each kid would approach us, remembering our name and beg again. Begging is their way of making a living for their family and is discouraged; however, it is difficult to pass by them. Some had replicas of the monuments that they would sell, as they asked for a "dolla".

On our trip to Copan we would always see people walking beside the road and children playing beside the road. There were different types of homes in this area, more adobe with thatched roofs. We saw the cultivation of coffee, tobacco, sugar cane, pineapple, bananas and oranges. There were fruit stands and firewood for sale beside the road. Living fences were everywhere. These are wires stretched between living trees that serve as the fence posts. We were stopped once by the police to ask about our travels, but were left to travel on. We also noted that the cattle have the right of way on the roads, as we were slowed by their presence.

Copan is quaint and small with a population under 5,000. It's in a lovely valley surrounded by gentle mountains. The streets are cobblestoned. We ate at a lovely restaurant attached to a hotel. After lunch we ventured out onto an upstairs veranda and saw a woman washing her clothes downstream nearby. Then we looked upstream and saw a man "doing his business" in the stream.

Sunday a few team members went to a huge Evangelical church in San Pedro Sula. The minister asked us to go up front of the congregation. Our lead optometrist spoke a little broken Spanish, and then someone from the congregation interrupted his speech and began to interpret for him. The service was in Spanish with beautiful singing. We found out later that the congregation was expecting some founding fathers to visit, and thought our VOSH team was their expected guests. Non-the-less we got an unusual welcoming at the church. Later we visited the artesian market with everything you would want to purchase as a souvenir as wood, cloth, paintings, Copan artifacts etc. Such a neat trip!

Returning from my first mission was a real reverse cultural shock. Seeing the poverty and need was heart rendering as I return to the States and get back into our spendthrift lifestyle. Preparing a Thanksgiving meal for my family was most difficult, as I thought of the street urchins and the people of poverty in Honduras. In the back of my mind, I was thinking about my next mission and returning to a third-world country when the opportunity would arise.

The Experience of Haiti
with a medical team

In 1996 Susie, my roommate in nursing, called asking if I would like to go to Haiti on a medical mission with a team from Upper Sandusky. This mission was sponsored by the Community Christian Center in Upper. The team would be led by a Family Practice medical doctor and his wife, a pharmacist. I jumped at the chance. The team members met prior to the actual mission, and after discussion it was felt that a construction worker would be needed with the medical team, as the Christian compound needed some renovations. I called my husband and quickly he said "Yes" that he would also join with the team. Preparation completed and in April eighteen people were anxiously awaiting departure from the Columbus airport at the early hour of 5 am for their adventure into Haiti.

Haiti is in the western part of the island of Hispaniola, which it shares with Dominican Republic, and the second largest island in the Greater Antilles. There are two sets of mountain ranges and is considered a Caribbean country. It is estimated that 11 million people live in Haiti, with a million of who live in the capital city of Port-au-Prince. The soil erosion and deforestation have caused flooding at times and the wash out of the top soil into the fish beds ruin the fishing for the natives. Water is unsafe for drinking and we were advised to shower with our mouths closed tightly. So off we go!

There was much luggage to handle, as medications and clothing were also taken to help the poorest of poor in Haiti. We were expected to leave our personal clothing in Haiti when we returned home, so too tight t-shirts were worn and other clothing that was not our best. As women, we were expected to wear a longer skirt with shorts under the skirt. (I found out later that this works well when you need a bathroom break in the banana fields). I chose slouch socks and sturdy high-top men's shoes. What a sight going into JFK airport in New York! Before departing in our small planes, the captain asked that we shift the most weight into the front seats, as we were loaded heavy and wanted to get off the ground. That was encouraging to start out! We flew American Eagle to the JFK terminal and experienced a very rough ride, as a weather front was coming in. Most of us were ill by the time we arrived into New York two hours later, and we applauded upon landing.

Thank goodness for transportation to get the team to the far concourse. My husband had gone through customs in Columbus with a carry-on containing a hammer, nails and all his tools; however, in New York these were taken from him. The airport allowed these items to be wrapped and shipped as a check-on as he went through the line. They really went above and beyond to help a carpenter be able to do his work in Haiti. We hoped it would arrive when we landed, and it did. We all got a bite to eat to settle our stomachs before traveling on. We found out that we were the last plane to land, due to the incumbent weather. Others were placed into a holding pattern.

The flight to Port-au-Prince was fairly good with some rough times due to the weather. We arrived a little late from our four-hour flight. Most passengers on this flight were Haitian, those going back home. One of the first things we saw was the presence of the UN protecting the airport. When we arrived the temperature was 91 degrees and stayed the same for the entire week. We retrieved our 36 pieces of luggage and surrounded it, as many other people were wanting to help us. Absolute bedlam! We brought with the team from Ohio a young girl named Pappillion. She had met Chad, grandson of the Director of Mission Possible, and he was living at the Christian compound where we were going. They had plans to marry; in fact, we later on attended their wedding back in Ohio.

Chad was a God send! Thank goodness for he and his hired helpers from the compound, as they loaded into the back of a cattle truck the entire luggage and all of us! On the ride to the mission we saw nothing but utter poverty, much worse than Honduras, as on my first mission. Tap-taps, small trucks with a covered bed used for public transportation, and trucks loaded with people. Goats roaming. We arrived an hour or so later windblown and wind burned from riding in back of the truck. We dodged pot holes and bumps as we went along, pulling in the extended side mirrors as we passed vehicles, missing people walking beside the road and animals on the road. Horns blaring!

The mission was behind an iron gate and the compound had guard dogs and a guard at night. I never found out how the dogs, one named "Boss", would not bother us, but if a Haitian came close to the beach, the dog would growl. The area was so beautiful here with green foliage and the Caribbean Sea nearby.

Our first meal was spaghetti and a salad. My favorite anyplace in the world! We had a cake to celebrate a wedding anniversary of some team members. There was a gorgeous sun set over the water. I can see why Haiti was once known at the "Pearl of the Antilles". We opened all suitcases and got our bed assignment. There was a men's and a women's dorm, each with four sets of bunks. We have generator power on, then off, and then back on again, but it kept the fans going most of the time in the hot, humid weather. We unloaded three piled tables of "stuff", clothing, and medicine everywhere. Finally to bed.

Today we travel to the Dupin school. The bell rings at 6 a.m. for a breakfast of bulgur (wheat cereal), bananas, honeydew and market bread. I never knew what market bread was until on our way home when I saw these small loaves of bread placed out by the roadside in a near-by town, ready to be purchased. Dust from the unpaved road was flying, as we drove past, covering the market bread. We packed the truck and off we go traveling an impossible dirt path crossing three river streams, ruts and numerous obstacles, poverty, naked children, utter devastation. It's so unreal to me. We set up clinic in the middle of the road, as we were unable to travel any further. There is a stream coming down from the mountain beside our clinic site and mothers would bathe their children in the stream. I was told that the Dutch constructed the stream for the Haitian people to get water from the higher elevations down the mountain. People at the lower end of the stream use the water that others have bathed in, as this stream of water is contained in a cement basin.

Children came to see us, class by class from their school. We see over 200 children. As the sun moves, we move our clinic stations out of its path. We have set up registration, temperature table, lung

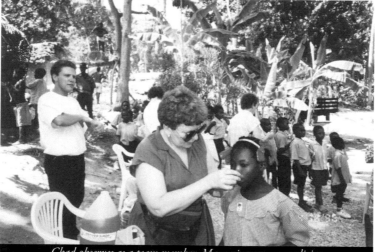

Chad observes as a team member, Mary, gives worm medicine

sound area, ENT and then the doctor exams the child. We finish our exam with a dose of worm medicine. I work in the pharmacy with Franswa. I wrote in my notes that I cannot describe my feelings today.

Our lunch was of market bread with peanut butter and jelly, bananas and water. We carry some of the medicines in plastic pans, such as those brought home from a hospital stay in the States. We emptied out two pans and on leaving our clinic site decided to hand them to some of the women nearby. A fight erupted as two women were trying to get the same plastic pan. They rolled on the ground and pulled hair as we were driving away. What else can I say?

My husband went with us today, probably he will be helping with the carpenter work at the mission compound after today; however, I was glad that he could experience one day of clinic. We ride back again in the truck to the compound for supper of chicken, rice and gravy with cake again. It was a time of reflection after supper and to bed early as we were very tired.

On Thursday we traveled to the school of Chardene. Our breakfast was chadezene, a cross between an orange and grapefruit, banana, and pancakes. Today we saw 237 children. I had a chair to sit on and worked with the pharmacy and Franswa again. There was singing by the helpers and a man played a guitar. The music and songs are always cheerful in Haiti, as we see such devastation and to me it would be despair. Today our clinic was set up under a mango tree and we kept out of the sun most of the time. Tonight our supper consisted of goat (my first time), rice and beans, carrots and militone, mango pie, gravy and salad with tomatoes. Very tasty. There is a couple from a local town back home that comes to the compound and spends their winter months to help. Another couple stopped in for a visit, they were from Columbus. Our team consisted of five RNs, a doctor, pharmacist and other occupations.

On Friday we visited the Baptist Haiti Mission east of Port-au-

Prince at Fermathe. The compound sent us off with a breakfast of Haitian omelet with tomatoes and onions, papaya, watermelon and toast and then we were off to Port-au-Prince. What a trip! We shopped at the Baptist Mission and bartered with the locals, then visited the Baptist hospital. A sign at the hospital indicated that firearms were prohibited. I took a photo thinking that was unusual, now years later I see a similar sign when I enter our local hospital here in the States. We viewed voodoo fetishes and charms at the Baptist Haiti Mission. Voodoo in Haiti is a composite of beliefs of many West African tribes and practiced by a few.

We were at a look-out point over 3,000 ft. above PAP. Then we traveled into the city. Masses of people were everywhere. We were told to roll up our windows, as someone may grab the watch off your arm, so we rolled up the windows. This day we drove about 150 miles and got back to supper of tuna and noodle casserole, green beans, salad, watermelon and mangoes. I am beginning to become accustomed to our surroundings and am getting over the initial cultural shock. There were some better houses that we saw today. I could see the two classes of people in Haiti, the poor and the very poor. We met other mission groups, one from Canada a group of 19 that were hand carrying in much needed medicines and supplies to hospitals. Many people want to help the Haitians.

Saturday to the Dejeance School…sounds of the morning – waves washing onto the shore, goats bleating, roosters crowing, bread fruit falling on the second floor tin roof, horns from the nearby road, and the guard dogs barking. Breakfast with rolls, watermelon and bananas. Off we go to clinic, a ride for a short time on the road, and then down a lane until we could no longer travel any further. We walked up the hills carrying our medicine and supplies in the hot sun. What a climb! We were joined by many children along the way. We then set up clinic in the school. I again worked pharmacy with interpreter Rosemond. At noon a mob erupted. Chad had an enormous job keeping them under control. He finally grabbed a plastic ball bat and hit a tree, getting their attention to get them lined up in an orderly fashion, as the door to the school was being pushed in. That was one time that I felt rather frightened. One child had an abscess in this upper thigh. One woman with a huge lower lip was treated. Otherwise there were many skin infections, gripes, worms. We saw 234 patients. We passed our worm medicine and vitamins. I felt that this treatment would only last such a short period of time, until another doctor came to visit the children, if that would occur. It was frustrating to me knowing that our treatment was just a short term fix. How can we help these lovely children in order for their life to be better? The trip back down the hills was steep and some fell, a very rough walk.

We got some stones between our tires that were pried out and we continued our trip home. Yesterday we saw about 15 people changing tires from PAP and back to the compound. Used tires were for sale all along the road, as with the many pot holes, tires didn't seem to last too long. Supper was ready when we arrived back by 6 p.m. We had red snapper, rice and gravy, broccoli, salad and cookies. The shower really felt good tonight. Water held on the roof warms by the sun and gives us warm water. Electricity off, generator on, making it almost impossible to sleep in the hot temperature.

The house over the fence next door was having a voodoo session. Many of the Voodoo houses are brightly painted; however, this one was not. People at the compound say the session will last all night. Chanting and lighting of candles are going on. A group of adults are lifting a girl wearing a long white dress up near the fire. A rather frightening ritual. We were peeking over the fence outside our second-floor dorm. Then the wind started to blow. My notes say…Will try to sleep, with our heads covered up!!

Sunday is church day in Monstrous where we received many

hugs upon entering the church setting. This is the Mission Possible Christian Academy and the largest school run by Mission Possible. I found a worm in my bulgur for breakfast, so that's the last of that for me. Some of our team members have a child to sponsor and so they met with the child's family. Three hour church service! Beautiful music. The tunes were familiar, however, with their French-Creole words. We went in front of the church to speak, all 18 of us. What an honor. Communion was given with the grape juice in small, plastic medicine cups. These were probably left by some missionaries. Back for lunch of chicken and noodles.

Some team members went to a local beach; however eight of us stayed here at the beach on the compound. The dogs protected us from the local Haitian boys. Lots of boy swimmers with no swim suits. A different life style here. We had a shower for Chad and Papillion. We plan to sponsor a child for a year, so we collected some things from the pile of clothes that were taken with the team and will meet with her and her family. It was kind of difficult rummaging through the donations. We are now on generator power and electricity has been off for a long time. Sleeping is difficult when the generator goes off in the 92 degree temperature, under a tin roof on the second floor. We have eight women in our dorm with one bathroom. We only flush when it is brown, and all tissue is placed in the nearby wastebasket, due to the system not handling lots of paper. If it's yellow, let it mellow. If it's brown, flush it down!

Monday again with no electricity, but we at least have water coming from the mountain to the holding tank on the roof for showers. Today we go to Sam's school and hold clinic inside. It is rather small and with the heat the body smells get rather strong. We saw 115 children then traveled to the Mission Possible Christian Academy to see children. Their kitchen serves 700 children bulgur daily. Some of these children may only have one meal a day. It is so sad for me, but the children appear to be happy. Our lunch today was of pumpkin soup and very delicious. One of our team members gave a ball cap to a little boy and later on this boy brought back a shell to give to our team member showing thanks for his gift. How thoughtful! These are tear jerkers that you find in Haiti!

We take off to Pier Piem to see a doctor, originally from Findlay, who has started a clinic there. This clinic is very busy with approximately 400 patients being cared for each day. They are staffed with 4 doctors and others. We then travel on to St. Marc to visit a hospital with various wards, pediatric, maternity, medical and surgical. We noticed patients being covered up, as they lay dead in the wards. Syringes lay outdoors in the dirt. A naked girl sat on the steps outside the pediatric ward. Children were seen with their black hair that had turned red and having bloated stomachs that were signs of malnutrition. We stopped at the post office and general store in St. Marc. What a terrible devastated city. On the trip home we saw the people doing their washing of clothes in a local stream. A long day and need for a shower before the generator power goes out, thus shutting down the lights, again a hot night with no fan.

Tuesday is our last day of clinic and we travel to a town with no name. They call it number 81. We saw 215 patients in this most utter despair of a place; some had come to us in wheelbarrows. One patient had a seizure and fallen into the fire and came to us to clean the burned skin. We set up clinic in a building that was so full of dust and dirt, we could hardly breathe. The worm medicine station was in front of the hog pen. Pigs, goats, cows and chickens were running through the nurse's station. I had a pharmacy station by the door and could breathe better. I tried to stay in the shade, as my rash from Doxycycline was present. This was taken for anti-malaria prevention. The first thing we saw when we arrived by truck was a little boy crawling with the mother sow and her pigs.

He appeared to be around four years of age and still crawling, but we noticed his one leg was twisted. We found out later that his leg had been broken, but never set, so now he crawls everywhere. We treated many skin infections with Ivory soap that we had brought with us from the States. My helper, Peter, said that if he could just have a cake of soap he would be so happy. To this day I cannot throw away the sliver of soap, when a cake of soap gets low in the shower, as I think of Peter and his desire for a cake of soap.

We eat our lunch of peanut butter sandwiches with market bread in these deplorable conditions. After clinic we distributed market bread that had been brought for the members of the community. We first were told to get up in the truck bed to hand this bread out. As soon as it was known that we were going to give out bread, everyone came running with outreached hands for the bread. It was indescribable. We could do nothing but cry! Can you imagine that we almost had a fight to get a piece of bread? If people in the United States could see what deplorable conditions that are present in Haiti, which is the poorest country in the Western Hemisphere, perhaps more consideration would be taken to consider help to the Haitians.

Passing out "Market Bread"

We traveled back to the compound in our 1½ ton truck in the back to see that my husband had hung a door at Pastor Antoine's house today. That might keep the animals out of the front door; however, there was no door on the back entrance, and the birds can still get in the windows without glass. Supper was goat stew and breadfruit, rice and beans. The compound was still on generator power which means no fans again. Chad has been a delight. Tonight he dressed up all in black with a mask and straw hat and crawled up on the flat roof on the second floor outside our dorm room. He shook the iron gate then quickly descended down a drain pipe. He came around to our door to ask why we were screaming. It was good to have some fun in this country of devastation. Movie night was around a 9 inch TV out under the cabana with the team and 50 Haitians watching!

Wednesday we were off to Port-au-Prince in the back of the truck again. Traffic was extremely heavy and we had long waits to get our 18 people through customs. My husband had bought a machete and of course that was the suitcase being searched. The custom agents were swinging it around and I thought that we might not be able to get it home. Just some teasing, as they repacked it to send the suitcase on to board the plane. What an experience! I'll have to think about this for a while. I vowed not to return, but that didn't happen, I returned in 2010 and again in 2015. Haiti grows on you and I would like again to return to the beautiful people of Haiti.

Return to Santa Barbara, Honduras for a Second Visit

Our team returned to Honduras in the fall of 1996 again to the Santa Barbara area with VOSH and again over Thanksgiving. Fourteen members of the team began their mission in the early hours of the morning on November 22nd, after overcoming many obstacles in packaging of the glasses, floods from the rainy season in Honduras and an expired passport. Our lead optometrist was carrying an urn with ashes of a child, who had been sent to the States for care and had died. The child that I was to accompany back to Honduras became ill and could not make the trip.

Besides the 9000 pair of glasses, the team carried medical supplies, clothing, toys and miscellaneous items for the children of Honduras. We first landed into Tegucigalpa, the capital of Honduras. This airport is one of five most dangerous airports in the world, in which to land. As the airplane has to circle around the city, that is surrounded by mountains on all sides, and then get lower and lower to approach the runway, which is short, before it finally lands. We felt that the left wing almost touched the ground as it made its last curve before touch-down. After a brief lay-over, we fly onto San Pedro Sula.

Our host had asked if the team would be able to bring some wheelchairs down to Honduras during our mission. So six wheelchairs were located locally and donated to VOSH, and some members of our team worked to make five good wheelchairs, which were able to be transported free gratis by the airlines. Having these wheelchairs carefully tied together made it easy for the team to transport them on to our clinic site. How surprised we were when we walked down the steps onto the tarmac and we found all wheelchairs untied and ready for the handicapped team members to use. We wondered what they thought when all the passengers walked to the terminal. We were easily taken through customs by our contact, the German Consulate officer for the northern half of Honduras.

Next we traveled to Santa Barbara in a church bus with Hernon, our driver and interpreter. We lodged at the El Moderno boarding house, as on our previous stay in Santa Barbara. Our meals were at Dona Anas, a local family restaurant, for rice, beans, fruit, tortilla, salad and pork chops.

On Saturday we set up clinic in the nearby Rotary Club in Santa Barbara. There were long lines of patients in the hot sun waiting to be seen by our four optometrists. Local interpreters assisted us with Spanish along with others, provided by our missionary host, Dolores. Our arrival was announced by a local radio station, this resulted in 320 grateful patients going through our clinic that day. I work with a boy named Roy. He teaches me Spanish and I teach him English. Our visit to Honduras was during the primary presidential campaign. We were able to experience the sights and loud sounds of a political rally and parade for one of the candidates, the only female running.

Team members and longtime friends Walt and John selecting glasses at the clinic

Visits to our host's home, with our care packages in the evenings, produced many needed and useful items for the children of Honduras. These items were provided by members of the team and/or organizations from back home. We had another member join our team on Saturday. He had traveled alone to join with us after obtaining a valid passport. We were sure glad to see him. We were awakened during the night by sounds of gun shots. These sound different than the usual fire crackers that are set off in the evening during this season. Dogs barking, roosters crowing are the other usual noises.

On Sunday morning we had time for the team members to visit the local market. Fresh fruit and vegetables, fish in buckets and meat hanging in the open air were for sale. Also hog heads were hanging in the market. We met the mayor of Concepcion del Sur during our walk through the market. We had originally met him on our '94 visit to Honduras, and what a surprise to see him again. Out of the fifteen team members for this mission, ten had previously joined VOSH for the 1994 trip to Honduras.

Our clinic on Sunday was at a school in the village of La Boquita. Driving back roads through creek beds and rough terrain, past fields of sugar cane, through washed out roads with mud and rock slides, we arrived at the school. There was no electricity. This was the rainy season and large rock landslides were on the road that we were traveling. We used battery hand-held auto refractors. A fuel burning stove was used to heat and shape the glasses frames. We saw many handicapped children with strabismus (three in one family), cerebral palsy, club feet and other medical problems.

Lunch at a beautiful local water fall provided enjoyment for the team. The walk to the falls gave us a close view of fantastic mountainous scenery and tiled roof homes with beehive ovens.

Our trip to the clinic site Monday proved to be a 2 ½ hour trip over bumpy, unpaved roads to arrive at the school at La Pulca. Every bump our tall optometrist hits his head on the top of the land-rover and leaves out a huge, deep laugh making the trip enjoyable. We lost 3 boxes of glasses off the pick-up truck, but fortunately they were retrieved by the members in the last vehicle of the caravan. These boxes were piled in with other team members in the back of the 4 wheel drive. We were packed to the limit! We proceeded over a suspension bridge, needless to say most team members chose to walk over the bridge. Frightening experience! However, on our return trip home, with a full moon, we were all so tired; we just stayed in the truck, weighted down with team members and equipment, hoping for the best as we cross the bridge. Arriving at the school, we still had many steps to climb while carrying boxes of glasses. Clinic this day cared for over 200 gracious patients. One little lady gave me a tightly wrapped present tied with string as a show of her appreciation. It was a small gourd that had been polished. I still have it yet today. At lunch time we ate our peanut butter and jelly sandwiches and then walked through the village. There we saw coffee bean grinders, animal hides being stretched out to dry, coffee and beans drying in front of the homes, people sifting chafe from maize and various animals roaming throughout

Villagers awaiting the eye "doctors"

the streets. A new medical clinic had been built on a hill beside the village. This was not open, however, medical personnel do travel to remote villages periodically offering care.

On the trip back home we traveled through the town of San Francisco. The church in the middle of town was quite impressive. The homes were quite impoverished. We continued our crowded ride with boxes on our laps for the long trip over bumpy roads.

I received a call at the El Moderno Boarding House from my daughter informing us that a good friend had died at a young age. She had tried four times and could only say "El groupo" and "Adios", unable to speak or understand Espanol. Luckily we arrived on the fourth and last call she was going to make, trying to contact us. I wanted so much to return home, but felt that there was more I could do in Honduras to help those in need.

We continue to have rice and beans for most every meal. Unable to eat the meat, as one jokester of the team keeps telling us it is "road kill". That night we walked by a full moon to the town square visiting a cabinet maker's shop, a furniture maker's shop and then to our host's home. The full moon, shining through the belfry of the church in the square, remains special in our memories of Santa Barbara. Pleasant evening. Each evening local shoe shine boys clean the mud from our shoes. These are the street orphans sleeping in a local church at night.

Tuesday morning we awoke to rain. Leaks in the windshield of the truck were duct-taped to keep us dry. A double rainbow appeared before our trip. A nice greeting to start the day! We traveled to Loma Larga, a desolate village with animals roaming freely. Most people and animals appeared to be extremely thin. The people of Loma Larga were so glad to have eye care available that they waited in heavy down-pours to get their eyes examined. Poverty stricken town! We saw 328 patients that day, many with bare feet as they walked through the mud and animal greetings.

Patients waiting in the rain

On Wednesday we traveled to La Canada. Rain and mud again. Again we set up acuity and registration on the porch of the school. We carried our own food, water and hand wipes to each village. There is no electricity. This day we used a charcoal burner to heat our frames for adjustment. It was a long day standing on cement the entire time.

We stopped at local homes constructing crafts, to make an income. In the evening we walked to a building in the town square in Santa Barbara where local dancers were performing typical Spanish dances. The girls were dressed in full, long dresses and the men in their tight britches. Later on the optometrists donated equipment for examining eyes to our host, along with leaving 8,000 pair of glasses for her to dispense.

Thanksgiving Day '96, a day I will never forget. We filled up the Toyota and off we go in a light rain to visit the caves called Tarule. There were stalactites and stalagmites, bats and spiders and lots of mud. In fact when you stepped into the mud, the suction would almost pull your shoes off. One member was hesitant to go on this adventure, as he said that once you have been in a cave they are all the same. How wrong he was!

We continue traveling to visit Lake Yojoa, one of the beauty spots of Honduras. This mountain lake is best known for its bass, making it a sport fishing center. We see fish hanging on tripods for sale along the lake. Back to Santa Barbara, we were driven to a lovely overlook to gaze down over the town, giving us a splendid view and then off to visit the local hospital's pediatric department. We were able to give stuffed toys and small toy cars to the 30+ children which were in the large ward. These children were in all states of illness, some appeared to be quite critical, with most cases being malnutrition. A nurse was bagging one child with oxygen to keep him alive. This was too much for me and I had to leave.

We visited the market to buy food for our evening meal, which was to be at our host's home. We met two exchange U.S. students at the market , one from PA and the other from NY, and invited them to join us for our Thanksgiving dinner.

We all traipsed into Dolores' home, mud and all. Dolores' home was filled with cribs and youth beds for the children she takes in and stays with her until they are well. She had adopted a 3 year boy, Jose, who had been living on the street, and we were enjoying playing with him, such a cute kid. What an enormous task for a woman in her late 60's. There were seventeen of us eating spaghetti on paper plates, some sitting on a children's chair or on the floor around the children's table. A Thanksgiving we will always remember and a successful mission with a great group of caring people.

Friday we drove into San Pedro Sula for shopping at the artisans market, dropping off Ziggy, a team member, to meet with a contact of his at some local restaurant. Ziggy said he had a package to deliver. We met him afterwards in the city square, and it seems that his contact he was to meet had a gun holster on his belt. Ziggy said he was just to deliver a package. We wondered what sort of mischief he was involved in and certainly hoped that our team would not be involved in anything illegal.

At our dinner we met Dr. Joyce Baker, a Honduras physician and a missionary from New York. Dr. Baker had been in Honduras for 30 years. She was originally from Defiance, Ohio. Much to my surprise we found out that her niece is my aunt. What a wonderful visit with a great lady. We have an enjoyable evening of conversation and good food. I had a "whole" red snapper for dinner, covering the head with my napkin so I couldn't see the eyes. We took left-over food to the street people sleeping on the steps of the large church within the main square. One woman was a wheel-chair patient, having lost her foot, living with the street people. This trip was too short.

Our Team Goes to El Salvador after the Guerilla War

After contacting the Rotary in Findlay, I was given information to provide VOSH safe entry into the country through working with the government. This was before the time that I had internet connection with our host, and a telephone call out of the country was so expensive, especially when you would get a person that spoke no English and I only knew a few words in Spanish. However, arrangements were made for this mission and actually the mission did go quite well.

We were to fly out of Columbus at 7 a.m. and found that three of our team members were unable to travel with us, due to family problems and one lost passport. At Houston, another member lost her ticket and was unable to travel on with the team, so we left her in Houston, not knowing what her next move would be.

So seventeen members arrived into the urban jungle of San Salvador, El Salvador and were greeted by the Directora General of Secretaria Nacional de la Familia for our mission over Thanksgiving 1997. All of the baggage arrived and we traveled by bus to visit the Artisan's Market, then on to see the Palace and the National Theatre. We were given special passes to visit the Palace and the National Theatre by the government. The National Theatre has huge columns that line the entryway, making the steps and area in between a favorite place for jewelry vendors to sell their goods. The courtyard of the Palace was groomed with formal plantings. These were beautiful, ornate buildings. The streets were crowded and almost impassible, but our host told us that not many people were here on Saturday! We viewed the extreme crowded conditions and the typical outdoor markets along the street where city dwellers get all their daily staples. We saw the Cathedral which was in the state of repair. This was where Archbishop Oscar Romero was buried after being gunned down in 1980 by the military. We saw a woman lying in the street with no one paying any attention to her, as cars would drive around her. We didn't know if she was dead or drunk. Finally the police came and carried the woman out of our path of travel.

Then we traveled to Suchitoto, our destination for clinic sites. We were escorted to Suchitoto by the police after dark with lights flashing and sirens blaring for the two hour trip. We had heard of banditos stopping travelers after dark, so we were extremely happy to have the police provide safe passage. We arrived into Suchitoto as a commercial was being filmed, with the lighted Catholic Cathedral in the background, and a live band for the colorful dancers. The church had been built in 1675 and this is where our official photo of the team would be taken after clinic was completed. The typical Central American dancers, including a "dancing bull" were the performers. The bull was set on fire and fireworks were displayed. This was a great entrance for the team to see local customs upon our arrival. We traveled on to our hotel, La Posada. This hotel was fantastic with a lovely restaurant, El Obraji.

El Salvador is a beautiful country with mountains and volcanoes ranging to over 7,500 feet in height. The colonial city of Suchitoto has buildings reflecting its Spanish rule. However, we did see bullet holes in some buildings from the 12 year civil war that was from 1980 to 1992.

We were to hold our clinic at the nearby hospital. We had a view of the war ruins of the hospital and a walk through the cemetery.

Our clinic site was to be held in a nearby therapy building, a nice secure area. We were much surprised when the team member, remaining in Houston, showed up with a police escort. She had purchased another ticket and traveled by herself, not speaking any Espanol, arriving into San Salvador. There she sat in the terminal until another person, unknown to her, greeted her speaking English. From that contact she was transported to our clinic site by local police. What determination!

Our host provided for the team a bus ride to a local falls and a beautiful view of Lake Suchitlan. We were shown around town seeing Galeria, a local church built in 1675, and a shop where maize is ground into flour and cooked maize goes into tortillas. We visited a local park and an orphan boy, Charlie, gave us a guided tour. It was so helpful and beneficial to Charlie also, as we paid him for his service.

We toured a local home being remodeled from war damage and heard stories how the guerillas drove through the town for 12 years. We were in an area not available for people to live in for many years. Supper was pupusas, cooked on a burner in the street. We chose the cheese pupusas, to assure our digestive system would

Team members ordering pupusas

remain healthy and we would be able to work the following day. These are also made with meat and/or beans. This is a typical El Salvador food. Interesting day!

We were greeted each morning by the local kids on our way to the clinic. During our 4 days of clinic we cared for 1,184 patients. Many had cataracts, glaucoma and accidental injuries to the eyes. These cases were referred to be cared for in the capital city of San Salvador. Others were helped with glasses. We had always handed out small American flags during our early years doing missions, and the children really enjoyed them. Later on in following years we began to be more cautious with this practice, as the anti-Americanism hatred was being spread around the world.

Our hotel had open windows covered only by bars. There were inside shutters; however, to get some breeze during the night, we left the shutters open. We were concerned about the mosquitoes and malaria, but no one became ill. We did see a huge tarantula on the outside porch. The maid told us not to worry, as we had nothing inside for the tarantula to eat. Little did she know that we always bring something to eat on our missions, just in case the food does not meet our palate.

Our team member, who arrived late, fell down some steps and sprained her foot on Tuesday. Now she was walking with a walker and unable to work. She had left her glasses at home, and couldn't see until glasses were provided for her. Another gracious team member appointed himself to care for her. If it wouldn't be for bad luck, she wouldn't have had any luck at all. She along with a teen-age girl were my roommates. I awoke one night around 3 am, and with the aid of the moon shining through the open window, I noticed that my accident-prone team member was lying in bed with her arms moving rapidly in front of her. I began to wonder what was going on. Later that morning I found out that she also could not sleep and decided to knit, by the light of the moon shining through the open window, while lying flat on her back.

A total of 6,000 pair of glasses was taken with the team, leaving the remaining glasses at the hospital for their use. We did have to turn away at least 100 people seeking care on the last day of clinic. This is always the sad part of holding clinics, when we cannot care for all the patients. With the help of our host, we were informed later that these people had been cared for by a San Salvadoran eye doctor, who set up clinic in Suchitoto and dispensed glasses from the inventory that we had left.

Prior to this mission we had held classes at our home for some of our local team members living close-by. We learned a little Espanol, at least enough to get by. Many of our missions would continue to be in Spanish speaking countries and we would refresh our language skills before each mission with a 10 week session taught by a local man who teaches Spanish in the schools.

Our group had brought 3 large boxes of clothing, books and school supplies and was able to deliver these to a local school. VOSH members were met by the school director and a multitude of children singing El Salvadoran folk songs. We always liked to provide items for the children on these missions, feeling that children may then grow up realizing that the Americans are caring people.

We were surprised as the First Lady of the country provided a fully-cooked turkey to the team on Thanksgiving, and sent it to the restaurant for our meal. The turkey seemed to be mostly brown meat, different than the turkey in the States, and was so delicious. What a wonderful gift to our team!

On Friday we traveled to San Francisco, a local village across Lake Suchitlan. This lake had been dammed up years ago, covering up many small villages. Twenty people traveled in 3 small boats across the deep lake, with no life jackets. We walked paths to the village, all up hill. We visited 2 homes where hammocks were being made. Our team members bought some hamacas and tried to carry them on their heads.

Due to time restraints our contact arranged for each member to have a box of chicken, Pollo Indio, to eat as we traveled along. Much to our surprise as we stopped for a traffic light, a pick-up truck pulled up beside us, loaded with freshly dressed chicken in the back of the truck. These were all uncovered and open to all sorts of dust and flying debris. We hesitated to continue to eat our chicken, but then thought well, it has been cooked.

We visited a museum and gardens and then to the Hospital Nacional de Suchitoto. We toured the hospital, visiting many departments, and noted that their wards were co-ed. We remained in the hospital for a reception in the evening. We all received a gift from the First Lady, a ceramic vase and a note signed by her. We enjoyed music and food of pupusas, nuegsdos, pastetes, and eupansdas. As typical with government, speeches were presented; interviews were held for the TV station and radio. A group photo was taken by our host in front of the town's Catholic Cathedral. We were told that VOSH was the first group to come to Suchitoto since their civil war.

Our last day was spent at Tesoro Beach in Costa del Sol, the "Coast of the Sun". Salvadorans come from every corner of the country to enjoy the beaches here. The beach was beautiful and clean, with strong waves and fine sand. While some members rode horses on the beach, the remaining team members picked up sand dollars and sat on the beach. It was very hot so the ocean and nearby pool was pleasant for the team. Plans were made for our next mission to care for the underserved around the world.

Nicaragua in 2000 after Hurricane Mitch

In 1998 I had a team ready to go to Nicaragua. Hurricane Mitch hit Central America three weeks before our planned departure date. Continental airlines said that we would have to use our tickets when they began to fly. They started to fly 2 days before we were to depart. I then had to appeal to Continental airlines and let them know that Nicaragua did not need eye care at this time, as they had much disease, floods, erupting volcano, mud slides etc. And our team consisted of a pregnant member and many older members. We all got our money back.

In 2000 we started our plans again for Nicaragua, with a few different team members and with a contact that lived in Miami. She was originally from Nicaragua and had family in the government. The problem was the Conservatives were in power with the Sandinistas gaining control, and our host was involved with the Conservatives.

This team consisted of 28 members. I read in my tour book… Managua grimier than grimy, uglier than ugly and hotter than hell. That was where we were going; however, only for a short time just to arrive and travel on. We arrived into Managua, capital of Nicaragua, and planned to travel to Estelí for clinics.

Upon our arrival into Managua we were welcomed by the Secretoria de Accion Social de la Presidencia de la Republica, and had an interview by the presidential private TV crew. This was late at night and we were a little surprised by the welcome at the airport. It was only the beginning of many political interviews of our team. We then traveled to a hotel, Maria la Gorda. This was a quaint, small hotel, just convenient for a quick sleep and to get up early in the morning. We had 5 men in one room with all the snoring going on, what a way to start our mission.

Esteli's name means "river of blood" in the language of the people who inhabited the area before the Spanish invasion. Esteli has seen more than its share of bloody violence during the years including the U.S. war on the Sandinista stronghold. The town is set in a wide valley 2,500 feet high thus offering a cool climate, much different than Managua.

Our first day of clinic, which was held at a local hospital, 3 TV stations were filming to use us as propaganda for the government. On the second day of clinic we crawled into the back of pick-up trucks to travel to the clinic site, we could not enter the enclosed compound due to lines and lines of people seeking free eye care. We had a visit from Jamilith Bonila, Minister of Social Action of Nicaragua observing our clinic. I was working with the auto refractor most of the time during clinic and when we went back to our hotel in the evening, we saw our team being shown on the news channel on the small TV in the lounge at our hotel. This was the only TV in our hotel.

On one day we cared for over 850 patients, our usual count being just over 500, with a total of 3,188 patients being seen during the week. We worked in a large auditorium in the hospital. This hospital had been recently built by the Dutch, a beautiful facility. We did have an opportunity to visit the various departments within the hospital. In the pharmacy, there were no medicines. In the laundry, there was no linen. Wheelchairs were held together with duct tape. The x-ray machine was inoperable due to a broken $5,000 tube that the hospital could not afford to purchase. It was

The editor using an auto refractor

then that the team began to think of how we could help these people. We even noticed on the one small TV in our hotel lounge that the government was pleading for supplies for the hospital. We did donate items to the hospital that had been collected from an area hospital back home, and presented these items to a doctor at the hospital. But this was just a drop in a bucket as to their needs.

We were asked if we would care for the prisoners from a local penitentiary, and we agreed, so we arrived early at the clinic site. These prisoners came to us in shackles and handcuffs with guards carrying M80's. We also examined the guards.

Our lodging was in a typical Central America hotel, Hotel Nicarao, where you have to share a bathroom with everyone and do not leave your soap, as it never returns again the entire week. I had to use shampoo to wash my hands. And the funny thing was that we brought large boxes of small soaps for the hospital and me with no soap. Guess I shouldn't complain as our bill at Hotel Nicarao was $12/day for a room and that included 3 meals. It just didn't include a cake of soap.

Actually the hotel was rather fun, as all members took up the entire hotel, even if it meant 3 cots in a bare small room with a shared bath. Or especially two men in a double bed that rolled to the middle. The patients knew where we housed, and a few actually came to the hotel for care. We ate our breakfasts and suppers in the courtyard at the hotel, under the open sky, on a long table.

We walked to the square of the town and bought ice cream cones after our evening meal. One of our members bought cones for the street orphans. They were so happy. We passed the food cooked on the street that all looked so appetizing; however, we knew not to purchase any if we wanted to be healthy to work in the clinic. I told one new OD not to try the street food, and after that time he called me "Mom".

We had a 9 piece mariachi band provide music for us one evening at the hotel and everyone was dancing in a Congo line. This was such a good way to introduce the Esteli Lions and new members of our team. On Wednesday evening the Lions provided a meal for the team, also having a mariachi band. Some of the members were pretty good dancers.

We were able to distribute school supplies, clothes and toys to an area school. These items were donated by churches and individuals from back in the States. We also brought some unused church bulletin covers and each child was handed out one piece of paper. How tightly they held onto this piece of paper. What an eye opening experience it was for us to think how much a piece of paper meant to the children.

Our Thanksgiving meal was at Hotel Nicarao, sitting at the long table under the stars. The Estelí Lions helped to host us and provided a fun evening on Friday evening as a farewell to the team. The work week went quite fast, and along with the assistance of the Lions, we completed a successful mission, caring for the many people and providing eye glasses to those in need. Patients were happy. Our host and the government were happy and we were treated royally.

Saturday morning we were having a tour of Masaya and the mercado. Masaya is known for its indigenous traditions, tobacco and rocking chairs. We were able to see many of the crafts at the mercado and purchase some souvenirs. Nearby is the active Volcan Masaya.

We traveled to the Nicarao Lake Resort by boat. There were Miss Central America candidates on the island. We listened to "woodpile" music. A government representative presented to each team member a certificate of recognition with our names spelled as "Doctor or Doctora". How we enjoyed these and I hung mine in my office upon returning home. The food was delicious. We ate a whole fish with the head still attached.

We then toured Granada. Once one of the grandest, richest, and most important cities of the Americas, the streets are packed with colonial buildings, making this a most architecturally vibrant town. We had met a man, Larry, while in the airport in the States. He informed us that he lived in Granada part time. So having instructions where to find him, we journeyed to his home and were given a private tour of his house. It was rather strange, as the woman opening the door informed us that Larry had hepatitis and was resting; however, we were welcome to see his home. It was filled with antiques from Spain. This was a beautiful elaborate home. We all wondered about this man's occupation?

We then returned to hot Managua to tour the city. We saw the Catedral Municipal, destroyed by the earthquake in 1972. It was beautiful with murals and statues. We saw the Plaza de la Revolucion, a rather new building. The Palacio Nacional was visited and is used today as a tax office. The exterior is decorated with huge portraits and the interior has murals depicting revolutions. We saw an army tank encased in concrete and rifles and weapons encased in concrete. There has been much violence in this country over its history and since the regional peace accord in 1990 the country remains calm.

Saturday evening we were invited to the home of the Minister of Finance, our host's brother-in-law. They provided snacks for the team and good conversation. The home was of the upper class, behind a large wall and guarded by dogs. This was indeed high living in comparison to the areas where we had been this past week.

Our last day in Nicaragua we were treated with a gift provided by the government of a day at Montelimar. This is a resort on Nicaragua's southwest Pacific coast, an all-inclusive resort with lush tropical flora. The Minister of Tourism presented to each team member a box of cigars, made in a local cigar factory, and a bottle of rum bottled in Nicaragua. When you have two members of a family on the team, it means there are enough cigars to provide for the entire neighborhood when you get home. We were bussed to the casino at Montelimar, known as Somozo's Hidaway and saw a stage show. We enjoyed a wide range of cuisine at the buffet while sitting near the beach. We swam in a pool that had a swim-up bar. Some members played chess with the life-size chess pieces. And we enjoyed the sunset over the Pacific. An end of an excellent mission at the Hotel Playae Barcelo Montelimar.

VOSH International later concluded that this was the target country to develop a permanent eye clinic due to it being the poorest country of the Central America countries. VOSH-Ohio teams returned again three times to hold eye clinics in surrounding towns and villages. An eye clinic was developed in Managua with the aid of VOSH International. However, in the long run, the clinic was disbanded due to the government placing too many restrictions and demanding too much money to bring supplies into the country. This is an example of corrupt government in these countries that try to obtain money for themselves and not to aid the poor, underserved persons.

International Service of Hope

The monthly trip to Waterville, Ohio continued by several persons from the Bluffton/Pandora area. From six to ten persons have volunteered in the warehouse facilities of International Service of Hope.

The monthly volunteering began on the Friday after Thanksgiving in 1998 when Hurricane Mitch postponed the planned VOSH/Ohio eyeglass mission to Nicaragua. The Bluffton/Pandora volunteers had been the most consistent group to help at ISOH. Most of these volunteers also serve on the eyeglass missions and at the Eyeglass Sorting Center in Pandora at the Pandora UM church.

Hospitals and medical personnel donate usable medical equipment and supplies to ISOH. People are needed to count, itemize and pack everything in cardboard boxes. These boxes are packed in large cardboard containers on pallets. The container/pallets are shipped throughout the world where there are medical needs.

Directors for the ISOH program travel to overseas locations to make arrangements for these medical shipments, and are often involved with coordinating the travel arrangements from foreign countries for children who are in need of operations or other medical needs.

A forty-foot Chiquita banana container was loaded at ISOH with about 33,000 eyeglasses from VOSH-Ohio, other medical equipment, hospital gurneys, examination tables, bed linens, nurse and doctor gowns, rubber gloves and medical supplies. This container was shipped to the main hospital in Estelí, Nicaragua. VOSH-Ohio places stickers all over the boxes to identify the donor and since the mission where the team members saw the need for supplies and equipment; we are hoping that this would arrive to its intended destination.

We were told that it sat on the border of Honduras and was unable to arrive into Nicaragua for months. If it ever arrived is unknown to us.

Venezuela 2001 under Protection of the National Guard

I worked with a woman, Julie, whose husband was a native of Venezuela. So when we were chatting one day, she suggested that we try to develop a VOSH mission in her husband's home town. This is how our mission began for Los Teques, Venezuela.

We had a warm welcome into Caracus, Venezuela, gateway to South America and the Andes, at 11 p.m. after our flight from the States. The son of our host and Julie's brother-in-law met us at the airport with a large poster created by the Graphic Design department of the oil company, PDVSA (Petroleum Division Venezuela South America). We knew then that we were special guests. And we were under the protection of the National Guard.

Los Teques is 40 minutes from Caracus driving the Pan American highway. It was founded in 1703 and the capital of Miranda State. It is an agricultural city with mountains and a pleasant climate. Colonial structures surround the Plaza Bolivar. Chavez was the elected president in 1999.

Our host was PDVSA, a government oil company where relatives of my friend were employed. This government owned company has some of the largest oil reserves in the world. The team visited INTEVEP, the research division of PDVSA and viewed films showing the company at work. This is the "brains" of the oil company, as all employees held advanced degrees of education, bachelor, masters, PhD etc.

We were treated royally. We stayed in apartments that were used by our host for their dignitaries while visiting. We didn't know how to act, as we usually stay in one-star lodging. We were under the protection of the National Guard the entire stay, every place we there, the guards were. After clinic we were locked behind a fence, behind doors, in our locked rooms. I was given a cell phone, walky-talky and gate opener to wear on my belt for communication during our stay. One member thought we would never be able to escape even in the case of a fire.

I was aware of peaceful demonstrations before we arrived and had talked to the Embassy. However, things got worse and three months after our visit there was a coup to overthrow the President, with the National Guard killing quite a few people and of course then Venezuela became anti-American. Our immediate hosts all lost their jobs from the company, as 2,000 employees were dismissed. Venezuela is no longer a place we could return.

On Sunday we were treated to a brunch at the country club and viewed the barrios built on hills surrounding the city. We visited a Murano glass blowing factory and were told that sand in this area resembles that in Murano, Italy where beautiful glass is blown. We saw Simon Bolivar's statue, father of the nation, during our driving through the city.

Our clinic days were held in a local hospital, Victorino Santaella, in the hallways on the second floor. Lines and lines of people went on forever outside the facility. Twenty-seven members including my friend, her husband and their 2 children were involved with working in the clinic. My friend's eldest son worked acuity and the six-year old passed out toys to the children on one day. Other days he visited with the grandparents. Our three teen-age boys with the team enjoyed the Venezuela girls who worked at the registration table and they became good friends.

Our host wanted to show the team the various cultures in

Venezuela. So on Monday evening we were taken to an Indian restaurant for our meal. Wednesday evening our host took us to their club for an evening meal and Thursday we dined at our host's home.

We were able to get unlocked for one evening to go to the "Mall". This was a beautiful building with a stream of water running through the middle, looking much like Venice with gondolas floating. I learned that Venezuela was "discovered" by Spanish explorers many, many years ago. When they landed on the coast of South America, they saw Indians living in stilt houses. The Indians were using boats that were shaped like gondolas. The country looked like Venice, Italy, so the explorers named it Venezuela, which means "Little Venice."

We split up into groups during our tour of the mall and noticed that there were guards in front of us and behind us with walkie-talkies talking to each other. So this was our free night, away from the National Guard, instead under the protection of police in the mall. And another funny thing was that we saw people who were familiar looking, as we had seen them during our breakfast at the INTEVEP center. We felt like the President, being so protected. And at that time we didn't know from what!

Since we were in Venezuela during Thanksgiving, our host invited the team to her home for a Thanksgiving dinner. There were 30 people attending. She, along with Julie, provided a turkey, mashed potatoes and gravy, a typical dinner for us. I sat beside a Venezuelan who thought this was such an unusual dinner, and I had to laugh. He did eat it and the team really enjoyed the meal. Our host's husband arrived home after a trip out-of-the country to see his house full of people, to his surprise. He was an intelligent, delightful person to chat with and the home was beautiful. Live flowers decked the tables and place settings were beautiful. It was a great Thanksgiving.

The city of Los Teques has over one million people, with much unemployment. The housing is quite poor, crowded on the hillsides above the city. Our host obtained for us to care for the poorest patients and those that had been affected by recent floods, those who were handicapped, and AIDS victims. This was the first volunteer mission that PDVSA had sponsored and our host was hoping that more could be established.

The VOSH team carried school and health kits, clothing and toys to distribute to the children on the last day of clinic. These were received with much joy and smiles by the children. We cared for 3,110 patients, took 8,000 pairs of glasses with us, and had to turn many, many patients away for their eye care. I stood outside of clinic site beside my host as she explained in Spanish that we could not care for the remaining patients. As they pleaded to be seen, I stood there and cried.

The last evening PDVSA provided a buffet meal and the National Guard members passed out their pins to each member. A choir performed Christmas songs and a plaque was given to VOSH expressing their appreciation for our work.

We spent one day with a boat trip to the beach on the western Caribbean coast, Falcon State. We spent time in the Parque Nacional Morrocoy. Mangrove trees were used as nesting sites for the scissor birds. Lines of red flamingos were seen at a distance

National Guard with team member Arliss

around the bay. We were housed in an apartment building that had been rented for mission teams. We had 6 people in a one bedroom apartment. Two couples slept in the living room. With all the snoring that was going on, I carried a cushion from my sleeping chair to the far end of the hall and slept on the floor.

Of all the elaborate housing in this area, we traveled through the impoverished areas of homes just outside the beach area. We were treated to an upper class mission with our facilities; however, we did care for the underserved and we began to see the two classes that are present in this country.

After we returned home I received an e-mail from our host telling us that the "skies have been crying since we left". Also she e-mailed about two years later asking if we could return; however, at that time no Americans were able to travel to Venezuela.

Poland 2002
My Favorite Mission

In arranging for this mission, we found many issues with customs. Many forms were filled out with required information. In our donation form there were questions as how many glasses, type of glasses, location of manufacturer (this needless to say was not answered, as you would have to look on each pair of glasses to see if they were manufactured as Italy, China etc.). I was informed to work through the Polish Embassy located in Chicago and mailed all information there. Just a few days before departure I had not received confirmation for approval of our mission, so I called the Embassy. Thank goodness, the man I talked too found our forms lying on a desk, and also told me that these should have been sent to New York. However, he said that he would pass them through and if I didn't receive confirmation before we departed for the airport, he would drive the forms to the Chicago airport. They did arrive shortly before leaving.

Thirteen VOSH-Ohio volunteers met at the Columbus airport to begin the first leg of the eyeglass mission and trip to Poland from June 5-20, 2002. Eight others joined the team in Chicago. The longest leg of the trip by LOT, the Polish airline, was direct to Warsaw, with a forty-five minute flight onto Gdansk.

Upon our arrival at the Gdansk airport we were welcomed by six high school boys with live-cut flowers. They helped load the 7,000 eyeglasses, optometric equipment and all personal luggage onto the bus provided for us. After an hour or more wait to get all items through customs, we proceeded onto our home base for this mission. Our delay was trying to get the glasses into the country. The Roman Catholic Parish, being a non-profit organization, did not specifically have "non-profit" in writing in their constitution. All forms that I carried to show proof of identity and donation were to be in both English and Polish. So to get the glasses into the country, our host obtained the non-profit subsidiary of the International Paper Company to act as the recipient of the glasses. Therefore a representative of the company had to be present to claim these glasses.

The Roman Catholic Parish of Kwidzyn and a non-profit subsidiary of International Paper Company were then our hosts. The bus transported us to the St. Benedict Convent in Kwidzyn, a city of about 40,000. Six of us stayed in the convent for the eight nights during our clinic time. Four others stayed in the St. Elisabeth Convent and nursing home, while the remainder stayed in private homes. The fact that a few team members could speak Polish helped much with communications.

We visited the monument to the Shipyard Workers while still in Gdansk. The monument was built after the famous Gdansk Shipyard workers' strike of 1980 and the creation of the independent Solidarity trade union. It was here where the Pope blessed the country upon its release from communism. We then traveled to Kwidzyn for our supper meal at St. Benedict Convent with more flowers and a visit to their flower garden outside the convent.

We arrived in Poland a couple days before clinic to see some of the area around Kwidzyn. On Saturday we traveled to the Malbork Castle. A castle of the Teutonic Knights which was begun in 1200 and took 150 years to complete. Knights wearing black crosses on their white cloaks were seen roaming the grounds. The castle was damaged in WW II and restored. This was a tremendously large castle with an estimate of thousands living there in its beginning years. There were sculling races going on the nearby river. And we were privileged to see some huge stork's nest built high upon tripod poles.

On Sunday we visited the St. Francis Church, sitting in the front row, as we were the honored guests. We visited the Kwidzyn castle, built in the 14th century by the Teutonic Knights. The interior of the vast cathedral has murals, early furnishings, Baroque altars and tombs. We visited the dudgeon in the attached castle and saw a torture box and various tools of torture. This castle was damaged in 1870; however, went on to act as a court, school, prison and now a museum. This area was ruled by the knights from 1243 to 1525. We walked the 200 steps to the bell tower and viewed the city of Kwidzyn with all the red roofs. We met with the mayor of the city at a music Festival and ate our evening meal in an open area by the music stage.

A clinic was set up for two days in Kwidzyn. It was located across the street from the 14th century castle. This castle would become such an enjoyment as I was able to play the organ in the huge cathedral and we also had a farewell banquet provided by the mayor of the city in the castle. To be able to play the organ located in an upper balcony, I needed music. So the sisters took me to their library. Books were in bookcases up to the ceiling, 12 foot high. I picked out some Bach music that was easy to sight-read and provided a small concert for our mission group. I also got up very early one morning for the sisters mass and accompanied their singing on a small organ in the convent. The singing was beautiful as we would wake up early to listen. It seemed like the sun was coming up at 3 a.m. each morning and our room had a large window. The farewell banquet was flowing with live cut flowers and recognition for the team of a job well done. I received for the team a metal statue of the Polish Eagle. Carrying this heavy object home through customs, wrapped in clothing, was interesting as we landed in Chicago and went through customs and having the usual luggage check. The man checking our luggage had a good laugh at what he discovered in the suitcase.

The six school boys not only helped transport the glasses, but they helped set up the clinics and served as interpreters also. Twelve high school girls joined the group also as translators. Together, all were outstanding with their assistance in the clinics. This endeavor helped the students with their English, as it helped us with our translation.

On Monday we saw 556 patients at the Kwidzyn clinic. On successive days, clinics were set up in schools or public buildings in Rakowiec, Gardeja, and Ryjewo, located within a radius of about 20 kilometers. These rural villages are considered to have from 65 to 100% unemployment. Patients were retired by 30 to 40 years of age due to the country recently coming out of communism, and no work was available for them. Our five optometrists examined a total of 3,192 patients, most of these patients received glasses. Our host had done a pre-registration process which helped with the flow of patients. No mob scenes, as has happened in many countries. Wednesday at the Rakowiec School, the kindergarten boys and girls presented a singing, dancing program for the team. It was so nice.

During our stay in Kwidzyn, the Catholic nuns, other parishioners and hosts provided several group meals, breakfasts and food at the clinics. One evening meal included a tour and dinner by the International Paper Company, which was held in a 16th century home of the knights and now Hotel Bealy Dwor-Podzamcze; another meal was a thank you dinner by the area health officials; and again a reception by the Kwidzyn city officials, which was held in the castle. We enjoyed a bar-b-q Saturday evening with all the types of Polish sausages, even some blood sausages. The food was prepared and served so elegantly. There were always fresh cut flowers and candles to dine by. The Father would play his accordion during or after our evening meal. One time we got one of our Polish team members to dance with Mother Superior. What fun, as the sisters were all laughing, including one sister who was over 80 years of age. I decided at that time the best place to spend retirement would be in a Polish convent. The sister who looked after our teammates spoke English. She would wait up until we returned home in the evening and offer us milk and cookies before retiring. It couldn't get any better than that.

Our last evening the city officials held a farewell elaborate banquet in the castle. Flowers were everywhere and we were presented with two of the most beautiful bouquets, that later was given to the convent and the nursing home. We were given books and each member received a certificate of appreciation. What a wonderful send off for the team.

After the week of clinic, we left our main luggage in the convent and traveled by train to Krakow, Warsaw, Sopot and Gdansk. Our send-off that morning with the sisters and Father was rather sad, knowing that we may never see these wonderful people again. The sisters gave each team member a rose from their rose garden, along with a hug and kiss. The Father played his accordion and our Polish team member danced with the sisters out in the driveway one more time.

Traveling by train proved to be beneficial, as we were able to see the country side of hay doodles and the typical housing and farms. This was the first time I had seen the graffiti on the train cars, which I now see here in the States. Many historical events occurred in this area throughout the centuries. This included the September 1, 1939 attack by the Germans at Gdansk, which was the start of World War II. Some of us visited the war memorial at Westerplatte and all visited the memorial at the site of the shipbuilders' uprising, that was under the leadership of Lech Walesa in the 1990's, before starting the clinics.

Some visited with trepidation, the former concentration camps at Auschwitz and Birkenau. These are two Holocausts internment sites near Krakow. We also visited the 1,000 feet deep 700 year old salt mine of Wieliczka, where miners had sculpted figures, chapels, and wall murals from the salt several hundred years ago, walking down the 400 steps to the 1 ½ mile underground we wondered if we would have to walk back up. Many weddings are held in the Chapel of St. Kinga in this salt mine as of today.

Historic buildings and architecture was surrounding us to enjoy. Krakow was a wonderful city and a city where much of the pomp and circumstance of the king's coronations and festivals were held. The castle on Wavel Hill on the Vistula River was a splendid place to visit. The near-by Cathedral of Saints Staneslaw and Waclaw is the most important church in Poland, with its royal burial chapels, it looked like it was made of pure gold on the inside. St. Mary's church in the Old Town Square played an unfinished Trumpet Call hourly to honor the man that was killed by an arrow while he was playing this song. The Old Town Square, with its pigeons and local musicians, was laid out in 1257 with the Cloth Hall, a gothic trade hall of the 14th century, which now holds a café where we ate our lunch. We visited the Florian Gate, Ulica Florianska, once part of the Royal Route that rulers rode from Warsaw for their coronation into Krakow. Now the artists show their paintings in this area. Wonderful place to visit in Eastern Europe. At this time there were not many tourists into Eastern Europe; however, over the years this has changed and people can appreciate the beautiful, old buildings and history that surrounds them.

Warsaw was also a great place to visit. We stayed in Old Town apartments both in Krakow and Warsaw. Both those in Krakow and Warsaw were on the top floor with 8 flights of stairs to climb, as no lift was available. These were relatively inexpensive and we had reserved them through the internet. We were a little apprehensive, as in Warsaw the apartment manager requested our passports and held them during our stay. This was an old communistic practice that had not yet been changed. We could house up to six members in each apartment and would share a bathroom. The apartments would be located within walking distance from the downtown Historic area. In Warsaw we could look out our window and see the Jewish Ghetto where during WWII the Warsaw people held-out against the invasion of Germany. The area was devastated; however, it has now been rebuilt in the same architecture as before the war. We then traveled on by train to our next and final stop.

Our visit to the Baltic Sea and Gdansk, seeing all the amber that at one time were the jewels of the kings, walking along the shore, riding the commuter train into the city, made this a memorable mission. The Sopot resort on the Baltic Sea had a pier 1,680 feet long, the longest in Europe. As we rode the commuter train into Gdansk red poppies grew wild along the tracks. We visited the Oliwa Cathedral and saw an organ built in 1763 by the monks, claiming to be the largest 5 manual organ in Europe at that time. We walked through the Golden Gate in Gdansk, constructed in 1612 -1614, and visited the market and walked along the Ulica Mariacka, Gdansk's finest street as it terminates on the riverfront.

Many of our interpreter friends visited us one more time in Sopot and Gdansk, as our young people brought our luggage to the airport for our return home. It was there we said good-bye to Poland, one of my most memorable missions and fantastic missions ever.

I tried 10 years later to arrange a return visit to Poland with our existing host, but could not get this completed. It was such a disappointment to many members.

Perseverance

Honduras 2003 into Juticalpa and Tegucigalpa

O ur previous host in Honduras was no longer coordinating missions at this time; therefore, we contacted a local missionary and were given a contact at a school that would sponsor the VOSH team. We were appointed an English-speaking employee of the school and it was here where we developed a wonderful relationship with Danny. Danny, our American minister, helped us as we visited Juticalpa, with the mud streets and poor, poor residents and then to Tegucigalpa to a school-based clinic. This was our third mission into Honduras, a beautiful, but very poor country.

Prior to our mission we prepared school kits for the children in the schools where we were going. Items were collected by various churches at home. This was a time when we were able to carry extra luggage without much cost involved.

We arrived into Tegucigalpa and were bussed by our host, the Holiness Evangelical Institutes, to Juticalpa. Juticalpa, "place of snails" is the major town of the Olancho department and was noted to be the Wild West of Honduras. We arrived earlier than clinic time, so we enjoyed a drive to Catacamas to visit the Talgua Cave. We ventured up a walkway to see human bones dating back to 900 BC. The cave was known as "The Cave of the Glowing Skulls" because of the way that light reflects off of the calcite deposits found on the skeletal remains found there. The site has gained the interest of archaeologists studying cave burials of Central America. Returning back to Juticalpa, we stopped at a roadside restaurant and enjoyed a Tilapia whole fish, including the head.

We set up clinic in a church and many patients were seen; however, there were many that we turned away for lack of hours in the days. Three of the team members were teen-age boys, one being our grandson, Jacob. What an eye-opening experience for the youth to see the poverty in these third-world countries.

The Christian School system had 6 schools and we held our clinics in 2 of the school districts. We were awakened by roosters and the call of a caged parrot kept by the hotel owners in Juticalpa. This was the only hotel in Juticalpa. One couple had a problem when she leaned on the sink in the bathroom and it fell off of the wall. Water was running everywhere. We finally found the hotel owner. He hurried to the main valve outdoors and shut off the water. What a mess. We met with local Lions club in that area during one evening. Lions are always friendly all over the world. Many of our team members are also Lions.

I saw a woman begging along the street. Danny explained to me afterwards that she had been married with 6 children. Her husband and 5 children were all washed out to sea during Hurricane Mitch in 1998. Now all she could do was to beg. You see many tragedies. People who walk on their ankles from club feet not corrected at birth, crippled unable to walk and much more. Health care is never like we have in the U.S. This was our last Thanksgiving mission as we switched to January starting in 2005.

We distributed the school supplies to the children in Juticalpa. We then traveled from Juticalpa to Tegucigalpa by bus after dark, when the brakes failed while driving through the mountains. We were told that this is a place where banditos stop vehicles. Needless to say, we all sat quietly in the bus for a couple of hours until another bus came to rescue us.

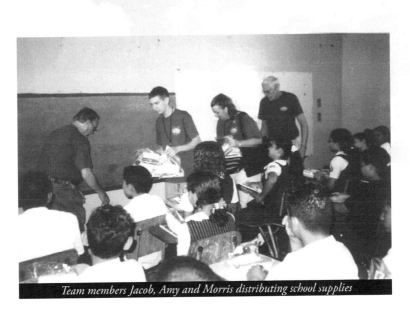
Team members Jacob, Amy and Morris distributing school supplies

In Teguc we stayed in a Christian compound and one couple found a scorpion in their room. We all had to take photos of the little thing, making a close-up really look bigger than it was. Clinics went well with interpreters from the school. Many patients were cared for. On Thanksgiving we ate rice and pork with a salad and Jell-O for desert. Danny took us to a bowling alley where the team also played pool. Friday evening we went to downtown Teguc and enjoyed fellowship outside a restaurant, while we bartered with the locals as they tried to sell their paintings to the team. We visited the Valle de Angeles before departing for home and were able to purchase souvenirs. Our last meal with Danny, the team decided to give him some gifts of what we had remaining with the team. His gift package consisted of toilet paper, sunglasses and a multitude of left over breakfast bars etc. Leftover food was taken to the homeless on the street.

We were a team of 21 members on this mission working with Danny. We asked Danny what we could do to help the school after we went home. He was hoping to start an English library, so for a year after returning home we collected children's books and mailed them frequently to the school. There was a bag rate through the post office ensuring that the books would arrive by boat, probably a slow boat to China, but they did arrive and the school had a great start for a library. Funds for shipping were provided by various organizations and new books were provided by our local newspaper editor, along with used books from organizations.

Danny moved from that position and has now become a minister and we met up with him for another mission in 2012. He has visited us a couple of times in Ohio with his family, as he returns to the States for fund raising. He is originally from Louisiana and moved to Honduras with his missionary family when he was fourteen. He came to the U.S. for his college education, and then returned to Honduras where he married a native woman and they have a sweet, little girl. More fun with Danny and his family in 2012.

Tanzania 2005
the Dark Continent

The planning for this mission was with the help of a Lion native from Arcadia. What a response from around the U.S. We had 14 optometrists sign up for this mission and decided to divide into two team locations for our clinics, and then meet up after clinic time to do a photo safari. Our combined team of 35 members jelled together well. I went with the Tanga team up into the mountains, which was a little cooler. The other team stayed around the hot capital of Dar es Salaam. The Tanga team provided care in the most desperately poor hospital that I have ever seen. There was no running water available. We were in a highly mosquito infested area. As soon as it became dark, all hospital patients lowered their mosquito netting over them. The children's ward had many deaths from malaria, along with malnutrition. Our combined teams met for a safari and trip to Stone Town, Zanzibar which was quite interesting.

Whow! What an amazing mission. I consider it a privilege to be part of a good organization, great teams of workers, and a privilege to provide a worthwhile service to such grateful people as we found in Tanzania.

Preparations for each mission were somewhat different. Working with the Ministry of Health for Tanzania meant that their requirements included a temporary license for each optometrist. Actually I found out while in Tanzania that the Dar es Salaam

Lions paid $50 each for these 14 OD licenses to practice for 4 days.

The Dar es Salaam Lions, which had 6 clubs, made arrangements for clinic sites, transportation, food and assisted with the clinics for the team in that area. This was the first time ever on any mission that our hosts were allowed to greet us prior to going through customs into the country. I also found out afterwards that one Lion worked to get this accomplished, by paying for this privilege. How money talks in these countries.

The Tanga Lions group was a small group. They assured that the regional health director in that area was notified, provided clinic sites and made arrangements for housing for the group. We met with the Lions group for an evening meeting and were asked to provide the blessing before our meal. Remember that most all were Muslim and we, being Christian, were a little apprehensive to respond. Upon departing from Tanga we never saw any Lions for our entire stay. Our drivers did not know where the clinic was to be held and I remembered that my host e-mailed about a hospital, so we drove to the government hospital and saw a sign saying "Welcome VOSH Chicago". So taking that meant us, we stopped and set up clinic.

The Tanga team loading glasses and supplies

I worked with the vice principal of an optometric school in Moshi, Tanzania, to get two of their students and an instructor, to work with one team in Dar for the week. I met with the instructor in my hotel room, as he was asking for money to pay the expenses of lodging, food and transportation. He asked for $500. I was shocked, as we were staying in a $12/night hotel, the food was being provided by the Lions, and our transportation by bus was to be around $6/person. I negotiated down to $400, much to my dismay. I just had the feeling that we were "rich Americans". Upon returning home I received an e-mail from the vice principal asking that they also be included with any clinics if we return for more missions. An ophthalmologist was provided by the government to work with our Tanga team. I believe he learned much from our optometrists.

We took 12,000 pairs of glasses on this mission, as we were supplying two teams. Airline tickets were a challenge to obtain, as many people were coming from different locations and we needed to arrive at our destination at the same time. Also some people wanted to return home at a later date than the two times being offered of Jan 27 or Jan 30. Immunizations to Africa included: Update Tetanus, Typhoid, Yellow Fever, Hepatitis A and Hepatitis B, polio booster, and malaria medication. We were ready to go.

Tanzania is located in Eastern Africa bordering the Indian Ocean between Kenya and Mozanbique, and is slightly larger than twice the size of California. The total population is around 36 million. It is composed of 99 percent native African and 1 percent consisting of Asian, European, and Arab background. On the mainland 30 percent are Christian, 35 percent Muslim and 35 percent other beliefs. Zanzibar is more than 99 percent Muslim. So, here we were, half-way around the world, a few light-skinned faces amongst many dark ones, and a definite reversal of experience for most of us.

Our 35 members with 9 ODs from Ohio, 2 from CA, 1 from TX, 1 from WA and 1 from CT were ready to go. The Dar team had much assistance from the Lions groups in their clinics and was dined after clinic times sometimes up until late in the evening. The Lions in Dar were Indians, spoke good English and provided their special Indian food for the team members.

The Tanga team had to do much on the spot arrangements for food, translators, etc. We basically worked from morning until dark, ate our evening meal and socialized with the team members then retired to our rooms. We had no entertainment as our host basically left us on our own. This was a first time for me not having our host with the team; however, the team members were great and we worked well together, helped each other and became friends.

While our teams were still together before we started clinics, we visited the fish market in Dar. This was an interesting place on the Indian Ocean. It was quite smelly, as the temperature was between 92 and 100, very hot and humid. The Indian Ocean is known as the Haven of Peace. We were provided transportation to tour the capital city and to visit the culture center. Young men climbed the trees to cut coconuts for us to drink the milk and eat the coconut meat. Native dancing, with drum music as accompaniment, was provided for our enjoyment. I was escorted by our host, Shanti, to exchange money with his personal banker and the exchange rate was $1 to 96 Tanzania shillings. I went into the bank with a large money bag and came out with a suitcase.

The Tanga team traveled 4 hours north to meet with our hosts. Along the way we stopped for a bathroom break. The bus pulled over on the road-side. The women walked up a path into the bushes. The men stood in front of the bus with their backs to us and we Americans took photos of our ODs, on their bathroom break.

Our hotel for the night was near a mosque where at 5 a.m. we heard the Muslim wake-up call. This occurs 5 times a day, but the 5 a.m. call was all we needed to rise bright and early. Since the team pays for their own expenses we go quite conservative during clinic times, and this hotel was quite conservative, with three of us crawling into our beds that were almost touching.

An extra pick-up truck was requested from our host to carry the glasses; however, it had been canceled, as our host felt we could load luggage on top of our 24 seat van. We looked like a bunch of gypsies going down the road. The 24 seat van held our 19 people, our carry-on pieces of luggage, and instruments and was to provide our transportation for the next 5 days. I rented the van for $400, but when I went to return it, I was asked to pay $1,000, as the owner indicated since luggage had to be placed on top, it would cost us more. I again negotiated down to $800 and don't know if he was happy or not. I told him to bill the remainder to our Tanga host, since he had made the arrangements. I did receive an e-mail after returning home from our Tanga host, saying that if we would return again he would try to do a better job in preparing for another mission.

We dropped off our personal luggage at the White Parrott Hotel for our 2 nights stay. I ordered lunches for the group to be brought to the clinic site and we headed on to the clinic site, as no one knew for sure where we were going. This was a government hospital. The government was remodeling the wings, as some were freshly painted. Some were not. As I mentioned earlier, no water in the hospital and the patients were not provided any food. A patient gets fed when a family member brings food in. When I walked into the maternity unit and saw a spigot I turned it on and nothing came out. The nurse saw me and poured some water from a pitcher for my hands. I wondered where the water came from.

I visited the pediatric ward on the last day of clinic, as the head physician wanted to show me around the hospital and also provide

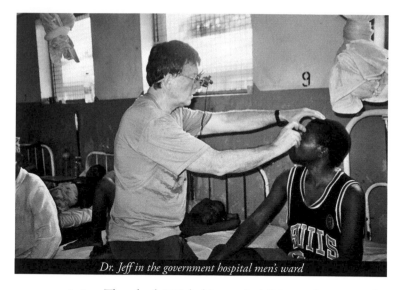

Dr. Jeff in the government hospital men's ward

some statistics. They had 333 babies and children admissions for one month, 97 were malaria cases, and there were 15 deaths. The ward had probably about 30 single beds and on each bed there were 2 mothers and 2 babies, except one single bed held 3 mothers and 3 babies.

We took care of our first Maasai patient dressed in their usual attire. We would see many more Maasai later on during this trip. As mentioned earlier the government supplied an ophthalmologist for the clinic. Actually we had 2 with us for a few days. One hooked up his equipment with an extension cord and all of a sudden we saw fire following the cord across the floor. Quickly it was unplugged. Having the ophthalmologists made it nice for our referrals for surgery. There was a significant amount of eye pathology that was identified by our optometrists, and either it was treated on the spot or referred to the ophthalmologist for additional testing and follow-up at a later date.

In all of Tanzania there are 122 tribes of Africans, all of which have their own language in addition to the official language of the country which is Swahili. We found that a significant number of people also spoke some English, lucky for us, as appointed interpreters were very limited. At the government hospital we had a couple of nurses help us, and at a clinic set up later in the public building we didn't have very many interpreters to help. We were fortunate to have a team member, Don, who had lived in Tanzania for 2 ½ years as a young veterinarian, and much of the language returned to his memory.

We marveled at the beautiful and riotous colors of the native dress. Each person although quite needy came with their own best clothes to the clinic. They represented a spectrum of backgrounds from Maasai, to retired school teachers, and businessmen. The men's ward in the government hospital held many men in traction. The traction consisted of rocks tied into rags; these were held up by ropes. We were asked to exam a few patients in this hot, crowded men's ward. Multiple iron single beds lined the walls with approximately one foot space between each bed. Some patients had IVs in glass bottles hanging. Our deepest fear was contracting TB in this close proximity.

Lushoto, our second clinic site, was called the Little Switzerland of Africa. Africa has such different landscapes – the bush country, luscious grass, mountains, the plains, pleasant scenery, fertile ground and poverty. The market place in Lushoto was a place of poverty. Our lodging was in Lushoto at St. Eugene's Hostel high up in the mountains. This was a Catholic training center and traveler's hostel in a very scenic location. I was awakened at 2 a.m. by a team member who could not find his Imodium. First I must mention, I could not get out of my mosquito netting, and then I couldn't find the telephone. In fact I didn't realize we had a telephone in the room. After this delay we dug out some Imodium from the suitcase and took it to our team member. It was much needed, as he declared that his explosive diarrhea hit the walls in the shower. Being awake I listened to the talking drums. First drums from one area, then a response from another area far away. It was breathtaking to be able to experience this. In the morning we listened to the sisters as they were singing during early morning mass in this peaceful place on earth.

Clinic was held in a community building. This was the first mission for one of our optometrist' wife and her request to me was to guarantee a rest room at all clinic locations. I could not guarantee this, but there was a building behind this community building with a hole in the floor for her use. I did not have the necessity to use it; however, when she went into the building she said it was so bad that she decided to go out in the grass behind the building. A true VOSHER! Our ophthalmologist did not have an ophthalmoscope, so VOSH donated one to him. We also left another ophthalmoscope back at the government hospital, as they did not have one in the hospital. Patients had not been scheduled for this clinic in Lushoto, so an automobile with a bull horn went through town to announce the arrival of the team. It did work to get patients, as we were busy and cared for many poor people.

The Dar team conducted clinics in the outskirts of Dar es Salaam in the villages of Mbuyuni and Kigamboni. Together both teams cared for approximately 4,000 patients over the four days of clinics. After our clinic days the group reunited for a photo safari trip to Lake Manyara and Ngorongoro Crater. It was here that we experienced the Maasai people and their way of life. The Maasai in the rift valley and Ngorongoro Crater area are known as the fly people and live in the fertile plateau. Their warriors are lion killers. The men of the Maasai at the age of 4 or 5 have 2 central lower incisors removed to allow for feeding in case of lockjaw. At the age of six they have their ear lobes pierced, at puberty, they have circumcision without anesthetic. They then become junior warriors. At about 20 they become senior warriors, at about 27 they become junior elders and can marry. In their 30s they join the ranks with senior elders and in old age are cared for as retired elders. On death they are put out in the bush to be eaten by the animals.

They are known as fly people and many flies surround them, as they dwell in their bomas, or huts made of dung. We had the privilege of visiting into one of their bomas and sat around a slow burning fire on which a pot of stew was cooking. There were two cots in the small 8 x 8 boma, one for the father and his son or sons and another for the mother and her daughters. Two small goats also lived in this house. One goat kept nipping at our team members; as we listened to the Maasai explain their customs. He had been educated in the U.S. and chose to return to his native life style, except now he could speak English. This group of Maasai allows visitors into their village, as we paid for this privilege, and they display their tribal dances of greeting for the visitors. Maasai are known as tall, nomadic people who follow the grass to graze their animals. Their wealth is their goat or cattle herds,

Lake Manyara National Park is known for the elephants, flamingos and birds. Ernest Hemingway describes it in his book "The Green Hills of Africa". Ngorongoro Crater is an extinct volcano with a rim about 8,000 feet all around it. It is a most famous wildlife refuge in the world. It belonged to the Maasai before becoming a national park. The government continues to let the Maasai graze their animals in the park and live close-by. About 20,000 large or moderately large animals live out their lives in the crater. We stayed in a lodge on the rim. It was the time of the full moon. I awoke at 3 a.m. one night and looking out of the large window in my room that faced the crater, I saw in the moon light a large cat like animal walk past my window. What an experience!

Earlier in the 20th century the crater was occupied by Germans and later by British farmers and squatters. In 1954 squatters were evacuated and in 1959 a conservation area was inaugurated. We saw lions, black rhino, elephants, wildebeest, zebra, water buffalo, eland, gazelle and warthogs. Termite mounds taller than men were abound in the park and also in the bush.

We traveled to Arusha, a tourist town for those coming to Mt. Kilimanjaro for a climb. We were mobbed by men wanting to sell their wares. In fact, I bought an article that I really didn't want, just to be able to walk through the mob. I later sold it to a team mate. Thank goodness I didn't have to carry it home with me. From this short stay we flew onto Dar es Salaam and then ferried onto the island of Zanzibar.

Zanzibar is a quaint place to visit. We saw a dhow that was used to carry anything from cloves or cement to chicken feed to corrugated iron. In the past many dhows were used to carry slaves to Asia, as this was one of their means of income on the island. These are beautiful crafts with their sails stretched into graceful curves sailing into the marbled blue Indian Ocean.

We visited the Marahubi Palace that was built by a Sultan to house his harem. It has since burned down many years ago, but we could imagine the 1,000 members of his harem and the ruins of their rooms and baths. We were informed that his favorite wife was kept in a house around the island and not close to the palace.

We visited the spice fields, still growing spices to ship around the world. Zanzibar ships 90% of the world's clove market around the world as of today. The slave market and trade existed for centuries; however, when the sultans came to Zanzibar, it increased. The British were instrumental in ending the slave trade and built the Cathedral Church of Christ on the site of the original slave market. There up to 300 slaves or more were herded and paraded each day in the late afternoon for the auction block. We saw a slave pen where a monument to the slaves had been placed.

Stonetown is Zanzibar's old quarter and not changed since 1850. You see traditional Islam clothing. Men in ankle-length robes and the women wear the long black gown. Embroidered caps are seen on the Muslim men. The women wear a headscarf only showing her eyes. The chance to visit this lovely island depended upon the safety at the time of our trip. We were fortunate to be able to visit, as no major incidents were occurring at that time. It was exceptional for me as we strolled the twisting, narrow streets from the market to our place of lodging. It was here that we ate our final meal together in Zanzibar overlooking the Indian Ocean.

From Zanzibar we continued back to Dar es Saalam and a visit to a Lions meeting for our farewell meal. Then it was off to the airport. We picked up our stored luggage from the $12/day hotel in Dar only to find that two of the pieces of luggage smelled like kerosene. Something had been spilled on them. We scurried off to catch the plane and only after half-way back to Amsterdam did a stewardess approach me and ask if I had something spilled in my suitcase. She checked it out and I saw the woman sitting behind me with a scarf over her nose. Evidently the smell went back and I didn't smell any fumes from the overhead bin where I was sitting. What a way to travel for 10 hours before she could get off the airplane. I had just purchased the carry-on suitcase for this trip and really liked it, so after arriving home I left it in our garage, scrubbed it, "fabreezed" it, and disinfected it for a year before I finally put a sachet inside and took it to the basement storage. It has been used many times since. What is so nice about this suitcase are its many compartments. I was so efficient on this trip to Africa that I had a small notebook and listed all the small items placed in each compartment. However, I then lost the notebook!

In all seriousness, this mission was a once in a life-time experience for me. Seeing the different cultures, the difference in people from one area to another, the changes in climate, all these differences as they blend together to make Africa a unique place to have visited. We accomplished our goal for clinics. We enjoyed our after clinic excursion. But as always, it was good to be home.

Perseverance

Ecuador, South America 2006 and Altitude Sickness

If you have ever been on a mission, you can understand the wonderful, fulfilling feeling that one gets from being able to help those less fortunate. When I joined with my first mission in 1994, I thought that if I didn't like it, it would only be one week out of my life. Since that time, I began to coordinate the missions, and actually live the whole experience from its inception, during the actual mission, and as I talk about our experiences afterwards.

I worked with a woman from Denver to organize this mission. She was a native of Quito, Ecuador and was invaluable to our team. She also enlisted the "Yo Te Amo" organization to act as our hosts. Both she and a representative from the organization accompanied our team into Ecuador.

We flew into Guayaquil, Ecuador in January into this hot climate, traveling along the Pacific Ocean on mud roads to the El Florin area, and were housed at the mission site of "Camino de Santidad". We were told to be very careful in Guayaquil, because it had a reputation for crime.

We caravanned to the four remote villages of El Floron, Montecristi, Los Geranios, and Canitas from the Manabí Province and held clinics in area churches. Our first day of clinic was chaos, due to patients pushing against the door to get into the clinic. Following days the patients were kept away from the entrance door and the clinic ran smoother. In Los Geranios we used a

Team arrives into Guayaquil with glasses, equipment and personal luggage

neighbor's bathroom across the road, as no facility was present at our clinic site. The bathroom had a water reservoir beside the stool so that you could dip the water from the reservoir into the stool for flushing. During our clinic in Montecristi, vendors set up booths in the nearby courtyard displaying their famous Panama hats, other straw items, and tagua-jut carvings. We observed the weaving of the Panama hats and needless to say, the team members helped the economy out during their stay.

Ecuador is a land of extremes. The lowlands which produce coffee, bananas, and rice near the sandy beaches and warm waters of the Pacific. The Highlands with their volcanoes and two mountain ranges cradle a high, fertile valley. The Amazon Rainforest occupies much of the country's land area. The Galapagos Islands are an ecological niche all their own.

Our clinics were all held in the lowlands. This was an extremely poor area with mud roads and small barren homes. Bakers in all the villages sent baked goods to the team as a thank you for their services. In Los Geranios, the school children sang to the team members their song of Gracias Senor.

Twenty-five members were in our team, with nine optometrists from Ohio and others from all walks of life, with the common goal to serve those in need. Our youngest member was 17 and accompanied by her OD father. A few were new members with the team; however, everyone shortly became an experienced VOSHER as the organized set-up at the clinic would provide the members a way to exam over 600 patients per day.

Travel was provided by our host in their camp vehicles. These were a 17 passenger van, a land rover, a pick-up truck without doors, and another extended cab pick-up truck. Luggage of glasses, instruments, and medications were packed in the pick-up trucks and at times on top of the van. Whoever sat in the front seat of the pick-up without doors came away with mud splashed on their legs. One truck had been rented and each day it would break down, and generally this would be on our way home from clinic during the darkness of night. We kept it in the front of the caravan, so if something fell off of the truck, others could pick up the pieces from the road. Our drivers were good mechanics and could fix the truck with the aid of flashlights held by the team members, and get it running again.

Our lodging was in the camp in cabins which helped to promote camaraderie among the members. The cook was great and we dined in the mess hall on meals of lots of fruit, rice, fish, chicken, plantains, and much more. Some members tried a local dish of guinea pig. We found that the caste system was still prevalent in Ecuador, as our helpers could assist us during clinic, but were not allowed to eat with us in the mess hall. Their place to eat was in the kitchen.

We arrived in the lowlands to a temperature of 96 F; however, a breeze off of the Pacific made it quite nice. Temperatures in the afternoons in the clinics rose well above 100 F but each clinic site had electricity and a few fans. The people crowded throughout

Optometrists rest at the camp after clinic

the villages anxious to receive the much needed eye care. The Ecuadorian people were so gracious and appreciative of their exams and new glasses. The team members were quite often getting hugs and kisses during the clinic times.

Our helpers from the native population consisted of some teachers and local people who either spoke some English or a few words. English is not taught in this area, so we were pleased to find those who could help us. Two American missionaries assisted us with translation. And our native Ecuadorian who moved to Denver in 2000 also traveled with us to assist in clinics and some sightseeing after clinic time. On our last day of clinic we gave away our ball-point pens to those just outside our clinic room, and what a rush of people came running to receive more. It was quite impoverished in this area.

After clinic time we traveled from sea level by commuter plane to Quito, which is approximately 10,000 feet in elevation. It was interesting to see a mountain poking its top above the clouds as we were beginning to land at the airport. We all had problems breathing immediately upon departing the airplane.

Quito was the host to the National South America Lions Convention during the time the team was present. We visited the Lions Club, their hospital, and eye clinic. VOSH-Ohio had previously sent 10,000 pairs of glasses to the Quito Lions in 2000 and the team was received warmly by their club officers. VOSH-Ohio again brought a suitcase of reader eyeglasses for their use in the eye clinic. The president of the Quito Lions Club invited the team members to a special concert and meal on Friday evening as their guests. Some of the team had altitude illness and were limited with their activity for a couple of days.

We visited the Old Town, unchanged since its colonial days. We dined in the Middle of the World, and stood on both sides of the equator to have photos taken. Nestled high in a mountain valley, Otavalo is famous for its outdoor market where locals wear traditional ponchos and beads, and specialize in the crafts of their ancestors. The team spent one day in Otavalo and arrived back to their hotel with many packages, of beautiful sweaters and crafts, tired from the travel.

The President of Ecuador was to visit the National Lions Convention on Saturday; therefore, Quito had police over the entire area around the presidential mansion and the Old Town. There was also non-violent protesting going on due to their $1.50 minimum wage. It got a little scary as we strolled through this area on our way to a restaurant Saturday evening. People with bullhorns were protesting in crowds and marching past our restaurant. However, the meal was wonderful and the two guitarists who played mariachi music for the group were well received.

Sixteen of the team members remained in Ecuador for an extension of 5 days after clinic to travel to the Galapagos Islands to visit this wonderland of tortoises, flightless cormorants, blue-footed boobies and waved albatrosses.

Guatemala Mission, January 2007, a Mission to Remember

Guatemala is at the top end of Central America, bordered by Mexico, Belize, Honduras and El Salvador. It has a small piece of Caribbean coastline and a longer stretch of black-sand beaches along the Pacific Ocean. Much of the country is covered by jungle and rain forest. Mountains are in the central and western parts of the country with the highest volcano reaching 13,800 ft.

When you list its assets, Guatemala seems to be one of the best travel destinations in Central America: the stunning Maya ruins at Tikal, the well-preserved colonial city of Antigua, a vibrant indigenous culture, active volcanoes (three are active) out of 33, highland lakes, exotic wildlife. But getting to these gems and enjoying them makes the country a challenge.

I worked with a local man who had lived in Central America and had now returned home in Ohio. He married a girl from Central America and they both had contacts where I could arrange for our mission. My contact was a Peace Corps worker living in the Mayan culture and he assured us that we would be working with the poorest people in this area.

The challenge was met by twenty-four team members traveling into Comitancillo, Guatemala, located into the Western Highlands. Team member's ages were from 16 to 79 years of age, a very close, cohesive group of individuals choosing the same purpose, to serve the underserved. One of our members arrived late, due to Chicago weather in January, and found that her suitcase was delayed. However, she caught up with us, hoping the suitcase would arrive soon. Another member was delayed in Houston, due to losing his passport. He did arrive later in the middle of the week.

The team arrived into Guatemala City and traveled on for an overnight at Lake Atitlan, with its enchanting backdrop of three volcanoes. Lake Atitlan is one of the most beautiful lakes on Earth. We stayed in the village of Panajachel, a well-developed tourism hub on the lake. We were able to exchange our money there with a rate of 7.5 quetzals to one U.S. dollar. It was here that one team member brushed his teeth in tap water.

From the 1950s until mid-1990s, the country's civil war was a deterrent to travelers. Since the war ended in 1996, the infrastructure has improved in many areas.

The ancestors of the Maya developed agriculture at some point before 2000 BC and became less dependent on hunting, fishing and gathering. Corn was a staple that allowed the Maya to develop. The ancient Maya civilization covered large areas of Mesoamerica. It reached its zenith between AD 250 and 800. Today, the Maya of Guatemala's highlands continue to practice many of their ancestors' traditions and beliefs.

Guatemala's recent political unrest can be traced to a 1954 coup, assisted by the U.S. CIA. A series of military governments then ruled the country and unleashed a campaign of terror in which thousands of people were killed and entire villages were massacred. In late 1996, the civil war ended. Over its 36 year history, the war claimed the lives of an estimated 140,000 people.

The following morning we traveled on to Comitancillo, stopping in Quezaltenango (Xela) for lunch and to purchase snacks for the week at the Hiper Piaz, the Wal-Mart of Guatemala. At that time we met with our travel agent who had arranged our transportation for the week. Our two great drivers, Lucas and Fidencio, stayed with us the entire week and assisted in the clinics as needed. These drivers took us through the curving, crazy, bumpy roads. The roads can only be described like something out of a Salvador Dali painting. This was supposed to be a seven hour bus trip from the airport; however, due to road construction, another 2 hours were added to the trip.

Quetzlatenango, also known as Xela (SHAY-la) is Guatemala's second-largest city. Built on the former site of a Maya city, Xela is an attractive place with handsome 19th century architecture. It also has several language schools. It was now getting a little colder at 2,330 ft. above sea level as we traveled on.

Comitancillo is located in San Marcos district in the Western Highlands. We traveled around 3 hours off of paved roads to settle into the town for the night. Our hostel, Pajaro Azul, was the only place to lodge in the town. Lodging there was quite rustic, especially on the last day of our stay, when the water was turned off in the entire town, due to a broken water line. We had brought with us our own sleeping bags, a towel, soap and toilet paper, as these items were not supplied by the hostel; however, the water, or lack of, was a problem. During the first of the week we did have water for showers, which were located outdoors for some of us. The hostel was multi-faceted, as some rooms were located inside and a couple of rooms had bathrooms. One couple shared a bathroom with 10 other workers at the hostel, as the hostel was under construction. Walking through the inside portion to get to the unattached group of rooms behind, motion lights would turn on and guide us through the maze. The rooms behind the main building shared the outside shower and bathroom.

With the elevation around 6,000 to 8,000 feet we found the temperature a little cool and that climbing slight hills made us short of breath. We slept at night with our heads covered up in our sleeping bags for warmth. In fact some people without much hair on top were wishing for a night cap. Bringing a sleeping bag was recommended by a Canadian dentist I had corresponded with prior to the mission. He said that we might need a sleeping bag to keep warm and to help protect us from the fleas in the hostel.

The lady next door was contracted to provide all our morning and evening meals in her home and they were quite tasty. She also provided bag lunches for us to take to the clinic sites.

Our host, AMMID (Association Maya-Mam Investigation & Development), provided interpreters from Spanish to Mayan Mam and 4 Peace Corps workers provided assistance from English to Spanish. We also asked another young man, a Canadian living in our hostel, to join us to help with translation in the clinics. He was spending 6 months working on a project in Comitancillo, with 4 months being completed at that time.

AMMID is an association of 23 communities in the Municipality of Comitancillo, whose principal objective is to facilitate, within the communities, the capacity to assess, identify, plan, implement, and evaluate their own development in a sustainable and self-managed manner. Their principal areas of focus are: projects combining agriculture and ecology, integrated health, production of handicrafts, and the promotion of democracy through education.

One of the most serious problems in these communities is the lack of medical attention, including vision and eye care. No government services of this kind are offered within their municipality. A cordial and respectful invitation to our team was offered.

Our clinic sites were as follows: Monday – Chicajala where we saw 430 patients with 18 referrals. Tuesday - Ixmoco 135 patients were examined with 4 referrals. Locals brought pots of food, carrying it on their heads, for the team members to share. We ate our lunch outdoors viewing the beautiful mountains and terrain. Wednesday – Tuichilupe 21 referrals with 236 patients examined and Thursday – Taltimiche 9 referrals and 144 patients examined.

Referrals were for mostly cataracts and pterygium; however, other conditions also were referred.

Most patients were older Mayan, with few children being seen. By going to the remote, mountain villages, the numbers of patients were not as high as in previous missions; however, every patient seen had not had previous care and there was a very high percentage of eye problems in most all patients. The optometrists felt that this was quite a successful mission and happy to be able to help these extremely poor patients. No patient complained if the glasses frames were not the newest style, as we have had in some past missions.

Referrals from these clinic sites have been given to Helps International. This organization will provide ophthalmologists to do surgery and the Peace Corps workers will assist in getting patients to the clinic sites.

While in Comitancillo, the team visited an organic farm being developed by a Peace Corps worker from Cincinnati. There was also another important project that the Peace Corps workers were involved with. This is the development of an inexpensive stove that the Mayans can use in their homes. At present, open fires burn in their homes and many burns occur, especially on young children, sometimes causing death.

More problems occurred with our team members as one member became quite ill, we assume from brushing his teeth in tap water. We had a Cuban doctor from town visit and he advised an EKG, due to a rapid heart rate. There was none available except 3 hours away in Xela. Our travel agency transportation refused to travel the mountains at night due to banditos. Therefore, the following morning the team member was taken to a private hospital, stopping every so often along the road during the 3 hour trip, as he became ill. He was admitted for a couple of days, given IVs and medicine. On discharge he was able to pay his hospital bill on his credit card; however, the doctor's bill had to be in cash, of which he had none. The ATMs were not working, due to the government having financial problems. Lines in the banks were long as the locals were trying to cash their payroll checks. So in order to get out of the hospital, the VOSH team arrived to pick him up and paid for his release.

Another member and her husband left in the middle of the week, due to her sister being admitted to a hospital with a severe heart attack. This occurred at the time when the team member with the lost passport arrived from Houston with a new passport. We still tried to get the suitcase from the airport in Guatemala City, with so many of our team members coming and going through the airport, but the airline would not release it. It was fortunate that we had hired a tour agency and they were able to transport the members to all the various locations.

We visited a local cemetery. There was still evidence remaining from the celebration of "Day of the Dead". At that time family members clean and paint the tombstones and provide food for the spirits. Balloons are then flown enabling the spirits to return to their place in the heavens as the celebration ends.

Our team stayed in Antigua overnight, just long enough to visit some of the markets and see the beautiful colorful Guatemalan textiles and of course to purchase some of their wares. Antigua's cobblestone streets and its preserved churches, convents and mansions were built in the 1500, 1600 and 1700's. UNESCO has named it a World Heritage Site. At this time Americans were able to adopt the children of Guatemala, especially the Mayan children. You would see some of the parents with their adopted children in the central park in Antigua. We were told not to take photos of the children while we were in clinics, as the parents feared that their children may be taken from them. We viewed active volcanoes as we traveled from Comitancillo to Antiqua.

Since my husband and I remained in Antiqua, following his recent release from the hospital, we offered to keep all extra luggages in our hotel room, while the remaining team members traveled to Tikal. The team was to depart at 3 a.m., and I asked everyone to be sure to obtain items that they wanted to carry with them the night before, so not to wake us up. Non-the-less there had to be a couple of the team members that forgot to obtain something out of their luggage, and we were awakened. We finally settled down. All of a sudden our door was swung open and a man was talking rapidly and loud to us in Spanish. We arose frantically not knowing what was going on. I could not understand anything he was saying. He finally left our room. We found out later that he thought we had missed our bus with the other team members.

The team then traveled by commuter plane to Tikal for 2 days of R&R to see the Mayan ruins. Tikal National Park is the most impressive archaeological site in the Americas. Although totally different in architecture and setting from the Inca ruins of Machu Picchu in Peru, it is just as spectacular. Situated in the jungle of northern Guatemala, the ruins occupy a large area about 10 square miles. So far, more than 3,000 palaces, temples, shrines, ceremonial platforms, ball courts, piazzas and residences have been mapped. Because this is a jungle area, it is hot and humid. Some team members rode on a zip-line over the ruins; unfortunately one member caught her finger in the pulley and found out after she returned home that it was indeed broken.

As we were ready to fly home our late-comer from Chicago picked up her suitcase at the airport in Guatemala City, along with a bag of glasses that did not arrive with the team. We all arrived home safely, after a much different mission than any previous ones, and anxious to see what next year brings in our plans for eye care to the underserved throughout the world. We often spoke about...if we survived Guatemala, we could survive anything!

Perseverance

Haiti house · pages 9-19

The precious children of Haiti · pages 9-19

The line never ends · pages 29-34

Team enjoying meals together · page 38

Our large team including host · pages 43-47

Kwdizyn Castle and Cathedral · page 51

Kindergarten kids · page 52

Saying our Good-Byes · page 53

Our Honduras team · pages 57-60

The Maasai standing in front of their houses · pages 68-69

The HARDY Guatemala team! · pages 79-85

Mayan patients · page 83

Romania team · pages 97-101

One of our many high-school interpreters · page 98

Women from a local village · page 100

Mexico team · pages 103-106

Haiti team · pages 107-114

Missionary flying service · page 108

Air evacuation on a cargo plane · pages 112-114

Presenting the PET · page 124

Patients come from outside the city · page 128

Romania team · pages 127-131

Patients crowding around the entrance door · page 135

The younger girls from the orphanage · page 137

Haiti team · pages 139-150

Children gather to pledge their flag prior to class · page 144

Elena and her husband, Cornel · pages 151-152

Some of our team members at the salt mine · page 154

View of the Carpathian Mountains out of the pension window · page 159-160

Haystacks abound · page 162

Romania in October 2008
Home of Dracula

When I mentioned to most people that our next mission was to be to Romania, their first response was "Isn't that where Dracula was from?" It's not impossible to forget Count Dracula, the Bram Stoker character inspired by Vlad Tepes, an actual 15th century prince of Wallachia. He is known to history as "The Impaler" for his ruthlessness to his enemies. Although history knows him as the demon in Romanian folklore, in Romania he is considered a national hero who liberated the country from the Turks.

Our gracious host for this mission to Romania was the Rotary of Targoviste. We worked with the Rotary in 2003 and sent in a small team for eye care and were anxious to return to this area again. The vice mayor of that city carefully pointed out to me that Romania is much more than Dracula, even though this

Count Dracula

image is skillfully exploited by tour operators, who organize visits to Sighishoara, the city of his birth, Bran Castle, known as Dracula's castle, and the capital of his kingdom in Targoviste.

Targoviste was our destination for October 11th, 2008. Arriving in our group were team members from Washington, Texas, Illinois, Missouri, New Jersey, Colorado, Kentucky, and of course Ohio as VOSH-Ohio conducted their 4th mission for this year. What a wonderful time to come to Romania. The weather was pleasant and the leaves were turning to their fall colors.

We had arrived at our destination after a long overnight flight into Amsterdam and then another flight into Bucharest with a bus ride to Targoviste. Prior to our arrival we had worked with the Ministry of Health to provide correct documentation to enter the country through customs without a hitch. And we did just that, because we found that customs were closed for the day and we walked straight through the airport. What a pleasant surprise!

We started out seeing the city of Targoviste, setting up for clinic, and going full force. After our first day of clinic when we examined over 600 patients, our host took us to a concert at the Music School of Targoviste. We were privileged to sit in the front row. The only problem was that it felt so nice and relaxing with a warm room and beautiful orchestra music. You can only guess what happened next!

Our host provided housing in a dorm at the Valahia University of Targoviste and our clinic was held in a large gymnastic room in the same building. This was an ideal setting to hold a clinic. We set up for our 4 ½ days of work and remained in this setting for our entire days of clinic.

Interpreters from the high school were provided, as English is taught in the schools beginning in the elementary grades. After clinic we were able to visit a local school and provide some books in English and German to the school. Our team donated books, school materials, and clothing for the children in the school and the underprivileged. We also made a visit to a day care center for handicapped children, where many of these items were donated.

VOSH-Ohio held a mission in Targoviste in 2003, and from that visit a friendship developed between Bill, our lead optometrist, and Dumitru Stefan's family. Dumitru again became our contact for this mission. A successful mission always starts with a good contact and this indeed was a successful mission.

Our team members melted together when newcomers to the group soon became old time VOSHERS, and we worked like a well-oiled machine as we processed 3,291 patients in our short time of work. There were six policemen who did an excellent job assisting with crowd control. The real challenge to the team came on Wednesday, when we were approaching 800 patients for the day. I walked out doors to see how the patient flow was going and saw that there were approximately 50 more people outside the fence. Then I found out that some of these people had stood there since 12 midnight, and it was now 4 PM. I was overwhelmed! Needless to say, we brought them into the clinic. It is so difficult to turn people away, even though the team may be to the point of exhaustion. We managed to see all the patients of the day and didn't lose the team either to exhaustion or to a walk out.

We had over 100 referrals, mostly cataracts. These were to be seen in a local hospital ophthalmology clinic. This was worked out through the Rotary. Our one problem that occurred during this clinic was the lack of glasses in certain prescriptions. We had 277 scripts that we were unable to fill. The Rotary contacted a young local optometrist, who was willing to work with our group and fit these glasses, if we could mail them to him. After we returned home, some members of the team pulled these scripts from the Pandora Eyeglass Sorting Center, and mailed the glasses to the Rotary. We had contact with our hosts, and received information that they were able to get the glasses to the proper patients. This took quite some time to complete on an individual basis.

Most of our patients were older, many into their 90's. All of course were most grateful to have the opportunity to have an eye exam and be provided with glasses, if needed. Besides receiving hugs, handshakes and kisses, we had patients bringing in bouquets of flowers to show their appreciation. One lady brought us a sack of plums, so ripe and so delicious.

Speaking of food, Romanians eat much slower than Americans. We had our meals served in the Theological Seminary. We were provided with a four-course lunch on our first day of clinic. Never-the-less, some team members were gone for 1 ½ hours for lunch, while the remaining half of the team carried on a "slow" clinic. That had to stop! We argued with the chief! We had to teach him the "American" style! The next day we were served buffet for each meal. They provided such delicious food. Tomatoes, cheese, cold meats and hotdogs, eggs, cereal for breakfast. Ciorba, breads, meat and sausages, potatoes, desserts for lunch. We can't forget the strong coffee! And for dinner we were taken into the city for wonderful meals. We experienced a typical Romanian dinner one evening, where we were offered a glass of plum brandy around an outdoor bonfire prior to entering the restaurant. Our welcoming dinner was a marvelous buffet with the Rotary. Our departing evening we were hosted by the Rotary again, only this time it was in a beautiful State House where the government houses dignitaries. We were served a fantastic buffet and a violinist entertained us playing "Turkey in the Straw" for the Americans. We felt like dignitaries!

When we completed clinic time we also were able to do the "Dracula" tour into the Carpathian Mountains to see some of the beautiful monasteries, castles and ruins as you will only find in Europe. The Peles Castle, Sinaia, is an example of the extravagance in architecture. Began in 1866, it is now a state museum.

The mysterious stone streets reveal slender buildings and houses that have ignored the passing of time and now display their beauty. Their charm cannot easily be described in words. We also did a day visit into Bucharest to see the National Museum, which reflects the history of medieval and modern times; the People's Palace, the second largest building in the world; and the village museum, depicting various architecture of homes throughout entire Romania.

Missions into this area provide a person the best of both worlds, an opportunity to provide services to the underserved, and to revel in the history and architecture of the old world. It was great, especially when our generous host provided us with personal tour directors, Ioana and Tony, from Stefan's family. Thank you, thank you!

As many of you readers know, team involvement means developing friendships that last a life time, both from the team members and those you work with in other countries. Some continue to correspond with their friends from all over the world, and these friendships are what make a VOSH mission so special.

Perseverance

Mexico 2009 during the H1N1 Flu Season and Drug Cartel Activity

This was a great mission into Patzquaro, Mexico. Our contact was the president of Cuidades Hermans Sister Cites de Patzcuaro. Besides the Sister Cites, the local government also became our host and provided in country transportation for the team as they traveled to the various clinic sites. Our contact also arranged a walking tour of Patzcuaro Historic Centre with anthropologist/guide Miguel Angel Nunez. Miguel was from a nearby university. And with this introduction we began to see the customs, culture and architecture of the indigenous people.

We worked through the government, as we understood of all the problems some teams had upon arriving into Mexico. We decided not to go through Mexico City, but to enter the smaller airport of Morelia. This happened to be the home of the drug cartels and much activity was happening in the news at that particular time. Along with the outbreak of the H1N1 flu, Swine flu, that had begun in Mexico, we had a limited amount of team members, actually 14 members, who were brave enough to participate in this mission. We had no problems with either the drug cartel or the flu. We had taken a thermometer and some masks in case of needing these supplies. We did ask one child to leave of clinic, due to coughing and a fever.

Entering through Morelia proved easy to get through customs; however, several bags of glasses and personal luggage did not arrive.

It took us 2 days to clear these glasses by sending all our paperwork to the customs department and then during the middle of the night I received this call in my hotel room with someone speaking in Spanish. All I could do was to arouse my team member next door who could converse with the individual. It turned out to be the man at the desk who called me, and he was just across the lobby from our rooms. After interpretation we found that the bags had arrived and were there in the lobby. So all of our preliminary work through the government did pay off after all, and we went back to bed.

Our work site of Santa Clara del Cobre, or "Copper Town", was a delight. In the past an individual with much foresight designated each of the villages around Patzcuaro to develop different handcrafts, not to be in competition with one another. Therefore you find ceramics, wood carving, needlework etc. in various villages. Santa Clara takes raw copper and fashions everything from earrings to bathtubs. Quite impressive. And we were hosted by the Paz family, owners of a copper shop. They so much wanted us to return for another mission into their town. Other villages were quite poor. Little old ladies with their aprons and shawls climbing out of the back of a Toyota truck coming to our clinic were seen quite often.

Many of the patients were illiterate, so in order to be sure that they were able to see after being fit for glasses, we would have the women try to thread a needle. This really worked to confirm proper fit of glasses.

We stayed at a hotel in Patzquaro in the middle of town, with a reduced rate guaranteed by our host. The town of Patzcuaro, on the south side of Lake Patzcuaro, has whitewashed adobe houses with red-tiled roofs, colonial mansions, cobbled streets and the smell of wood smoke in the air. The market place nearby was full of handmade crafts. We felt safe to walk the streets after dark in the square, as our host indicated that we would not be bothered.

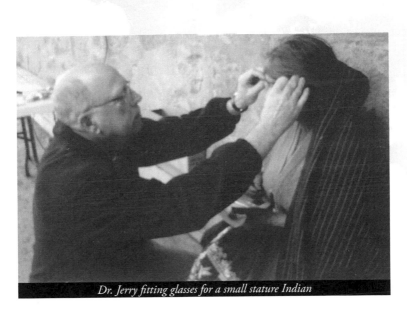

Dr. Jerry fitting glasses for a small stature Indian

Some of the residents of the villages are Indian and quite small in stature. In fact, a photo of my husband sitting showed him being taller that the little woman standing.

Our clinic days were different than other missions such as… arriving on Monday at 8 a.m. we found no patients waiting. Our host explained that it is early here in Patzcuaro. By 9:30 a.m. the place was packed and we cared for 325 patients that first day. On Tuesday patients arrived earlier and after caring for 522 patients, some were turned away. Wednesday was our day in Copper Town where we cared for over 600 patients and then the Paz family treated us to a wonderful dinner. Such great hospitality and appreciation for our team. They also presented each VOSH member with a copper plate with VOSH and their individual name hammered into it. I have it hung on my memento wall. Thursday we rode to Tzurumutaro, an old city inhabited by indigenous people, the Tarascan's. We cared for over 400 of these poor farmers. Friday we went into the mountains to Cuanajo with an altitude of 8,500 ft. The people are Purepecha.

Our rest and relaxation followed on Saturday and Sunday

when we took a boat trip on Lade Zirahuen, stopping by Santa Clara to shop. In the evening we walked to our host's home in Patzcuaro where she hosted an appreciation dinner for the team. Good traditional food was enjoyed along with an evening of music provided by ten men with guitars singing Mexican ballads. Sunday we toured the villages around Lake Patzcuaro.

These missions are so rewarding to the patients and even more so to the team members, as they get hugs from patients who could not see to read or embroider for years and now they can continue with their activities of daily living after having a pair of reading glasses. One Tarascan woman had ridden her burro seven miles just to have her eyes examined and returned home with glasses, now being able to continue her embroidering.

Air Evacuated From Haiti after the Earthquake 2010

Drums beating with people chanting in the night, roosters crowing, goats bleating, and the guard dogs barking. These are the sounds I hear as I lay awake in the early morning hours in our safe walled-in mission compound, wondering our next plan for evacuation.

I was a member of a 16 member optometric team who had just completed our mission work into SOLT mission compound (http://www.solthaitimission.org/). A mission we had planned with Father Glenn for the past year. VOSH-Ohio sends teams into underserved countries around the world to provide eye care to those needing these services, and this was our first eye care mission into Haiti.

This was a mission that saw 2,556 patients and provided glasses to many of these patients. Most all of the school children were screened and adults from the surrounding villages presented themselves to the compound to have their eyes screened for distance acuity, examination by auto refractor, a health exam by an optometrist, selection of glasses if needed, and fitting of these glasses. Those patients with surgical needs have been identified and will be referred for further care.

Now that the mission is complete, how do we get home? The most devastating earthquake in 100 years had hit Port-au-Prince this week, one that we felt there in Hinche 75 miles from the epicenter. After clinic on Tuesday, the team visited outside the walled compound to see the garden. While visiting, the earthquake hit Port-au-Prince. All of a sudden some team members experienced extreme vertigo. Not knowing what was going on, it was a strange sensation. We did not feel the earth shake; however, there were several bouts with vertigo. The carpenter member had remained at the compound and he reported the house moving and a calendar swaying on the wall. We soon found out of the mass devastation as Father Glenn invited the team over to his house to watch CNN. Calls from team member's families were being received by Father Glenn, along with their concern for the team. The news was terrible; I immediately tried to contact four people in PAP and was not able to find out their well-being. As of today, I still have not found out about two of these persons. As a medical optometric team, we have no supplies or organized talent to help those affected; however, the desire remains to help these people and our hearts go out to the beautiful people of Haiti.

Our stay at SOLT had been most pleasant in this country of need. Father Glenn had provided for our team delicious food, homemade bread, Haitian and Cajun cooking at its best, and his presence has enriched the lives of our team members.

This was a first time visit to Haiti for 12 of the 16 member team and a lasting remembrance is one of love and fellowship with our Haitian helpers in the clinic, members of the team at SOLT, and with the team members as we experienced our next adventure to depart the country.

The location of SOLT required that the best way to get into the compound would be to fly over the mountains to the mission. A missionary flying service provided four six-seater planes to lift the team from Port-au-Prince to the grass runway near Hinche. Because we carry over 5000 pairs of glasses, equipment, medications, and our own personal luggage, along with food for the team, our host sent a truck to deliver the supplies to the compound.

We found pleasant accommodations for the team amidst the poverty outside the compound. We were housed in men's and women's guest houses. We had cold running water and electricity. So the fans were welcome in the hot weather, along with the cold showers.

Father Glenn and helpers cooked our evening Haitian meals of usually rice and beans, along with his Cajun cooking. The second day two goats were butchered. Warm bread from the bakery, that gives bread to the children in the school, was delicious. The compound teaches 1300 children and feeds these children 2 meals each day. Lunches consist of cabbage soup or a stew. Huge gardens are planted to provide food for the children. Hogs, chickens, and goats provide meat and eggs. It is a well-run compound. Father Glenn has built 90 houses for the Haitians and set up an organized program for the owners of these houses.

Now as we were on our final flight to the States, it is still hard to believe what had happened this past week. We had to make a decision how to try to get out of Haiti. I called our airlines and rescheduled our flights. I was told they would begin flying in five

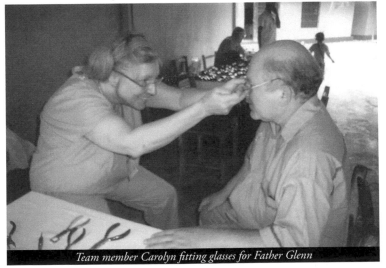

Team member Carolyn fitting glasses for Father Glenn

days and so I rescheduled the team for the first flight available, which was in seven days. Actually Continental did not fly into PAP for two months. E-mails kept coming in from family, friends, and organizations giving us advice on how to depart, as Father Glenn had electricity through the satellite. Options provided to us would be to try to cross the border into Dominican Republic, since the PAP airport was damaged. Then we were told the border into DR was closed. We were told to go north and fly out of Cap Haitien and get a lift by missionary flight services. This would be a five-hour trip in a tap-tap or chicken bus over unpaved roads to reach the port, and then a missionary service could get us out. Another option would be to have the missionary service fly into Pagnon, 13 miles away, to pick us up. Calls to the missionary flight service told us that they were only taking supplies and rescue equipment into PAP and would not offer their services to us for probably six days. Even though the border to DR was only a few miles away, it was cut off; going north was also not available for us. We felt we needed to get out soon. Reports told us of the unrest and violence in the capital city of PAP. The US Embassy recommended the U.S. citizens leave, and contact with the embassy provided that, starting on Friday, the U.S. would evacuate their citizens. This is our only option.

Quickly the team packed and we rented an air conditioned (meaning the windows open) van and started our venture. We decided that each team member must get out with only one suitcase. Glasses, medications, and some equipment along with all our duffels were left behind. Excess clothes, shoes, and personal items were left behind. We did take toilet paper, water, surgical masks, breakfast bars, and the team made peanut-butter sandwiches for the members, as we had no idea how long we would be at the airport until we were evacuated.

Luggage was piled high on top of the van and tied down with

a frayed rope. The van was supposed to hold sixteen and a front seat was to be used by a Haitian guard. Well, that would be sixteen Haitians, not Americans. Four persons were to sit across with a jump seat. No way! Our idea of taking a guard in the front seat was abruptly stopped. We put two team members in that seat and three to four across each bench in the back, assuring that the only two skinny team members were distributed evenly. During the three hour trip I could hear "If you move this way, I could move my foot or shift to this cheek".

Travel over this road from Hinche to PAP had recently been completed to cut an eight to twelve hour trip down to three hours. Haitian roads are mostly not paved and have multiple rocks in the road bed. We honked and swerved the entire trip to miss goats, horses, people, and other vehicles. The bumpy travel was extremely exhausting for the young as well as the older team members. Then our adventure began!

Arriving at PAP we were immediately in a traffic jam. All were trying to pass in the streets scraping vehicles just to get through. Fallen buildings, Haitians walking in mass, Haitians in tap-taps and chicken buses over-loaded inside and on top, heading out

Haitians fleeing Port-au-Prince

of the city with furniture, suitcases, chickens, and animals, etc. Haitians wearing masks, riding motor bikes with multiple people on each bike any way to get out. And we were trying to get into the city.

Our driver inquired about the best streets to take in order to get to the airport. Finally we arrived. We found the terminal damaged and the tower not working. We disembarked to a crowd of men wanting to grab our suitcases. I finally consented on 3 helpers, as all suitcases were tied on top of the van. Three were tipped much to dismay and shouting of the others. We were led through the fence to another exhausting part of our journey.

This was Friday at 12:30 p.m., 3 hours after leaving the safe compound. We were instructed to stay in line and stand, due to the terminal being unsafe to enter. We stood there for five hours, eating our sandwiches for supper and distributing our remaining food to the people through the fence, as we were on our way home shortly. The U.S. had soldiers surrounding the airport. We were safe and going home.

After five hours in front of the terminal, the team members were looking for a rest room. Men were instructed to stand between two buildings and women were allowed to enter a single very undesirable toilet within an adjoining car rental agency. We were glad to have carried toilet paper.

Then we were led surrounded by U.S. troops to go behind the terminal where many cargo planes were arriving and departing. The noise level was only shouting level. We were again told to stand in single lines. I think back to our five days of clinic as we had our patients "stand in straight lines". The only difference was the length of time we stood. Planes from all over the world were bringing in rescue teams, the dogs for body retrieval, all sorts of medical and rescue teams were arriving. Three patients with IVs were lying on gurneys on the tarmac waiting for smaller evacuation planes to arrive. We were interviewed by Portugal and French TV stations and some other radio station personnel. Again we stood for another five hours.

At 10:30 pm we were led out onto the tarmac to enter a U.S. Air Force C 17 cargo plane. Probably around 100 people were strapped into seats along the wall and down the center in the belly of this plane. We talked to Brian Williams and Ann Curry. Katy Couric was also a member on this plane. We were treated well by providing blankets, pillows, and ear plugs to help with the noise level.

I found out later that Brian Williams had televised over the Atlantic and I was in the background sleeping. My second claim to fame was being on National TV sleeping with my mouth open! This came up on You Tube and a team member was quick to notify me of my TV appearance.

We needed to stop in Charleston to fuel up and then on to McGregor Air Force Base, as they had been commissioned by the government to deploy the refugees. When we boarded the plane, we had no idea where we would land. Previous flights had taken people into the Dominican Republic and Florida. Now a disaster plan had been arranged with the Air Force base. Finally at 6 a.m. on Saturday morning we arrived and were bussed to the base. We had name bands placed on our wrists, given a health kit to shower, briefed by the air force personnel and taken to a gymnasium full of cots. We were provided food and telephones if needed to make arrangements to fly home.

I felt like a refuge; however, it was such a good feeling to be home, especially since my skills as a nurse to help others would be hampered in this situation. After obtaining airline tickets we were led into buses to take the people either to Philadelphia or Newark airports for departure home. A state police was our escort with sirens on traveling through each traffic light for our speedy hour trip to the airport. We arrived at our final airport and home by midnight Saturday, two hours earlier than originally planned from our original flight one short week ago into Haiti. So much had happened after that 30 second shaking of the earth that will be remembered by many people for their entire lives.

We found that this 7.0 magnitude earthquake killed over 250,000 people in the PAP area. These people were buried later in mass graves. Our plans to visit the Grace Children's Hospital were aborted, as the hospital was damaged in the earthquake and my contact for the visit had been killed. An orphanage, His Home for Children, run by friends was on the list for our visit also. This too was not completed. Their home was damaged leaving the entire 90 orphans and helpers to sleep out-of-doors for a period of time. It would be at a later mission in 2015 when we would be able to complete our visits to the hospital and orphanage.

Peru 2011...Into the Rain Forest

Here I sit in the Peruvian jungle drenched from the seasonal rains that have even curled my passport. We just completed our annual VOSH-Ohio mission into Iquitos, Peru, a land-locked city in the jungle. This has been one of the most strenuous VOSH trips in a remote area.

From Lima, Peru we flew 600 miles over the Andes to Iquitos and met with the local 22-member Lions club. The club house contained an immense room that was wonderful to work in and provide our 5 days of clinic. The people of Iquitos are warm and friendly and quite poor. We have received more hugs and kisses to last a lifetime, as they were so appreciative of the eye care offered. We provided care for 2,809 patients and had to send hundreds away. Due to the bright sun, many people had eye damage, and 300 patients were referred for further surgical care that will be provided by a surgical team in early spring.

From our local hostel we boarded motorcars for an exciting ride to Club de Leones. The motorcar is a three-wheel motorcycle with a rickshaw attached. I have never had such a "wild" ride with motorcars competing to arrive at their destination by quickly switching lanes, passing and driving anyway in order to get to another set of paying passengers. At the clinic we needed to pass through hundreds of patients to enter until they could finally line up, in a somewhat organized fashion. Our 10 optometrists

Wild ride in a motorcar to clinic

and other volunteers totaling 26 worked throughout the day in sweltering 90+ degrees of heat. Occasionally a shower of rain would provide temporary relief. The sun is bright and hot as we are close to the equator. Dengue fever is making headlines in the local newspapers and some deaths have occurred locally. We came back to our hostel one day after clinic to find that we were not able to enter. The management had chosen this day to fumigate the premises, due to cockroaches. We enjoyed sitting outdoors until the smell dissipated.

After clinic on Friday we attended a local market, known to be quite famous for thievery. We were instructed to remove our watches, rings and even ear rings if we didn't want to donate these items to Iquitos. As we entered, six local police noticed our arrival and accompanied our group. I have been in local markets in many third-world countries; however, this one had many different items of interest which ranged from hand rolled tobacco, coca leaves, jungle hog, fish from the Amazon, various "live" grubs and worms that are eaten, dressed chickens laying in the sun the entire day, along with small bananas, yellow potatoes, etc. Since it was the rainy season with high humidity and mud, it proved to be a unique experience. We then boarded dugout boats to ride on the river seeing stilt and floating houses. Some of our patients had come from this poor, poor area. These houses reminded me of the photos seen in National Geographic. People living along the river bathe, wash and have outdoor toilets beside their house emptying into the river. Our guide instructed us not to put our hands in the water either because of the pollution or the piranhas, he didn't explain the reason.

We were able to visit a local village as we traveled the Amazon, the longest river in the world, to our overnight stay in a jungle lodge. Here the local villagers showed us the talking drums and did their native dance. The women were bare-breasted and wore bark skirts, same as the men. A fantastic dance was performed dedicated to the anaconda snake. I did not want to see one of these in the jungle as we walked about a half of a mile in the rain from our boat to the village. During the day at the jungle lodge we were able to catch and eat the piranha fish, walk through the jungle seeing the medicinal plants (boots were provided by the lodge for all with the exception of one optometrist who wore size 14), take a boat

River ride in a dugout boat

out after dark and listen to the sounds of the birds/animals. We viewed the locals feeding the monkeys outside their kitchen, Pedro the parrot was entertainment, and occasionally you would see a tarantula cross your path.

Back again in Lima we traveled by Peruvian airlines along with cages of roosters. What a surprise in baggage claim to hear roosters crowing. We decided that instead of riding on a chicken bus, as we have in the past, we now have flown on a chicken airplane! Some of the team members traveled to Cusco, the Sacred Valley and Machu Picchu. We stayed in Lima visiting the capital city, a city of 9 million people. The Plaza Major has the presidential palace where changing of the guard happens daily at noon with much pomp and circumstance. Local crafts are plentiful everywhere much different than Lima, Ohio where I attempted to buy a souvenir as a gift for my hosts in Lima, Peru. Occasionally you may see an artesian Inca native selling her wares, consisting of alpaca. The San Francisco monastery contains catacombs with many skulls and bones and is a marvelous historical building. We were hosted by the Iquitos Lions during clinic days and also the Lima Lions welcomed the team, as we were staying in Lima for a few days. If you are a Lion, you

Team members take a jungle walk

are welcome all over the world by other Lions. What wonderful receptions and welcoming we all received.

Sitting in the Houston airport after a night flight, I think of the busy Lima, Peru airport where flights depart for all over the world. Now in Houston we are almost alone as all flights have been canceled due to the airport being iced in. I reflect on some of our adventures. We stayed in a rather bare hotel in Iquitos; however, the owners of the hotel accommodated us to the best of their ability and when we departed the cooks, the maids and busboys stood at the windows and door and waved good-bye to the team. Where else does this happen? How we had no toilet seats on the toilets in the clinic and so we purchased seats and they were not stolen during the week we were there. Due to gastric disturbances with some team members these seats were appreciated. We usually bring a clothesline to do some laundry, but back in Lima we could not find any place to attach the line, so we sent clothes out to the laundry. We could see a man washing the clothes on the roof outside our hotel window and hanging the clothes on the line to dry. When they came back our underclothes were ironed. We marveled at the fact that our outer clothes were all wrinkled due to being in a suitcase for two weeks, but our underclothes were pressed. So many little incidents like some of these make VOSH missions so memorable and the team members become close-knit members of the family.

Changing lives in Honduras 2012...

Volunteerism can change lives. VOSH-Ohio recently returned from an optometric mission into Honduras in 2012. This was their fourth visit, the first being 18 years ago. At that time we rode in the back of pick-up trucks into the misty clouds to the outlying villages and the groups of underserved people waiting for us to offer free eye care. This time we rode in an outcast school bus from the States, from the misty clouds on the upper ridge above Tegucigalpa, onto the narrow, winding streets going into the city. We also served the people of the beautiful, small village of Cedros. Years ago we felt pleased to see 300 patients a day. On this

Village of Cedros, Honduras

mission we treated 3,474 patients and dispensed 2,035 pairs of glasses. How wonderful these experiences have been.

Flying into Teguc again is an experience that gets scarier each time. The runway has been lengthened; however, we still have to circle lower and lower around the city that is surrounded on all sides by mountains, so the left wing seems like it is ready to hit the ground before we land. Whew! Many airplane accidents have occurred at this airport. Tegucigalpa with its million people is the most populated city in the country. You see many small houses crowded together built along the hillsides and it remains a poor country.

Team members for this mission were ages from 16 years to senior citizens, molding their personalities together and forming a well-oiled machine, working tirelessly to care for the many patients.

We were so fortunate to have a team member that helped our team with our failing auto refractor. In fact, he was the co-inventor of this instrument. Dr. Ben, Director of the Applied Vision Research and Ophthalmic Telemedicine with the New Jersey Medical School, originally from Canada, is now semi-retired and travels extensively doing research and mission work. In December 2011, he was in Saudi Arabia and in Somalia working with research on the early detection and management of Vision Threatening Diseases. When he first visited the Arabic Nations in the mid 80's – he saw mostly Bedouins, as well as children from Yemen.

This program was sponsored by the Kingdom of Saudi Arabia and included the introduction of his retinal camera (Ret-Cam) that provided a view of the retina equal to 120 degrees. Dr. Ben also brought a retinal camera for use on our mission into Honduras.

One Vision Threatening Disease is Retinoblastoma. This is a rapidly developing cancer that develops in the cells of the retina. This can be either heritable or non-heritable and is rare, affecting 1 in 15,000 live births. If inherited there is a mutation on

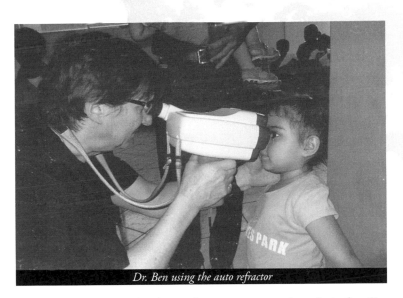
Dr. Ben using the auto refractor

chromosome 13Q1-4. The Bedouins marry within their families and it was there where Dr. Ben was researching. Having such an expert with our team turned out to be rewarding for our team, as one of our patients in Cedros was diagnosed with a Vision Threatening Disease. Immediately Dr. Ben e-mailed the retina images around the world to confirm his diagnosis and to find the best hospital that could handle the case. He received responses from as far away as Japan, China, Australia, Germany, Saudi Arabia etc. for a total of over 15 countries agreeing with the diagnosis made. Dr. Ben speaks many languages and has contacts throughout the world. It turned out that Tegucigalpa had a Pediatric Oncologist who could help this child. Time will tell the outcome, but at present all is being done to save this 4 year old's life.

Cedros was our first clinic site and is located a short distance from Teguc. The trip took a little longer due to a flat tire on our discarded school bus from the States. It is a mining town where the first constitutional congress of Honduras was held in 1824. It is a pretty, little town with cobbled streets and red tiled roofs. The only place for our team to lodge was in the school. Our host had provided bunks and floor mats for a men's dorm and a woman's dorm. Bathroom facilities were shared. Water was provided from a holding tank on the roof, and of course we ran out as the Americans were not used to going sparingly with water. A shower was set up in a closet with a heater, so the showers were warm, when there was water. You could go past the bathroom door that wouldn't close and see a man shaving, a woman brushing her teeth, and a man standing behind a partial stall door using the toilet. We became a close-nit family.

Our host cooked the food for the group. He was the pastor of a near-by church and such a gracious man. He would grill our food and we ate under a tent that our host had rented to keep us out of the full sun. Much fruit was available for the team along with meats, eggs and typical Central American food.

The children from the school were our interpreters and did a wonderful job. One evening the kids provided a program at the town hall with girls in long skirts and the boys wearing cowboy hats. Their dances looked much like a Spanish square dance.

We were also blessed to be able to present a PET to a 14 year old girl who had been crippled from polio and was unable to walk. The PET is personal energy transportation, a type of wheel cart made for those unable to use their legs. This cart is made entirely by volunteers throughout the United States and provided free of cost to any group that can provide the funds for transportation to a receiving individual. VOSH-Ohio shipped the cart to Honduras prior to the team's arrival. The girl receiving this cart had been 6 years at school; however, was unable to continue to the new school for the 7th grade and change classes. She is now able to continue with her education. She and her mother were so happy to have this provided to her by the VOSH group. Immediately she could drive the cart and made her way through our eye clinic set up in Cedros. Another life changed. See…. www.petinternational.org for more information.

The last evening in Cedros the team climbed up to a lookout over the village to view the sunset, the church and houses in the village. A local found some beer for the thirsty team members and what a wonderful way to say good-by to Cedros.

Our second city for clinic was held in Tegucigalpa, capital of Honduras. We worked in the church Casa de Oracion Familiar. Our long-time friend, Danny, was the pastor in this church and our host for this mission. Being in the city brought different clientele to the clinic. In Cedros the patients had not had eye care services and were appreciative of the care. In Teguc some patients had private care and were not too impressed with the glasses offered. This is one reason that VOSH likes to attend more to those in the poor, rural areas. Our auto refractor failed and Dr. Ben with his contacts was able to obtain a desk-top auto refractor from the local hospital for the two days of clinic. This worked quite well as it came with a printer and we were able to speed up the process of working the patients through in a timelier manner.

Our housing was in a Centre de Retires Iglesia Evangelica de Santidad with dorms again for men and women. For some reason we kept losing our shoes. We would go to sleep at night and in the morning, if we had two pairs of shoes beside our beds, only one shoe of each pair would be remaining. The men with tennis shoes began tying their shoes to the bed post. This was sure a strange phenomenon; however, the shoes did show up and we went home with the same amount of shoes that we came with. We never did find out who was the culprit.

Our host provided a day visit to the Parque La Concordia, a park that has a model of a temple at Chichen Itzen in Mexico along with some non-Maya statuary. This is also a botanical garden. We listened and danced to the music played by a Mariachi band. A grilled Honduran picnic was served and our host presented each team member with a certificate of appreciation for their service.

VOSH offers many experiences to those members volunteering. Honduras has proved to be a definite example of the VOSH experience.

Return to Targoviste, Romania with Visits to its Monasteries 2012

To start our mission off we had a 4 hour wait in Paris before traveling on to Bucharest after an all-night flight. When we arrived late into Bucharest we found that 2 team members, who were to meet us there, were nowhere to be found. Absolutely no information could be obtained from the airport officials. Our host finally contacted the Border Police and through them we found that our 2 members would not arrive until midnight, so the team headed to Targoviste with our other friends that would catch up with us later.

Our first mission to Targoviste, Romania in 2003 I did not attend; however, in 2008 I worked with our host and traveled to the clinic site. Our coordinator was excellent and we ran a smooth mission with good R&R to follow. So I was looking forward to a return visit to Targoviste and working with many of the same people as in 2008.

We had 5 new optometrists along with 2 experienced ODs. The team worked well together and many patients were cared for. We set clinic up for an entrance door and exit door. Then the exit door would not open, so patients were routed in and out of the same door. This creates a rather crowded situation in the narrow hallway. In 2008 we had 6 policemen to control the crowd. This time the Rotary members, especially Alexander a large German man, were our bouncers.

And keeping the crowd outside a fence made it easy. Besides the set up for entrance and exit being a problem, the patients had to walk entirely around the outside of the building, through a long hall and into the clinic site. Then when the eye exam was completed, the same route was followed. Mind you the hall was full of people standing to get into the clinic and the grounds outside the building were crowded.

I journeyed outside one day to observe the patients when a man with an apparent stroke was trying to walk the long path through the crowd. He was dragging his left leg and the left arm was hanging. Feeling sorry for him, I asked him to wait while I obtained a chair from inside. I then got one of our new ODs and asked if she could treat the patient outside and she agreed. However, the sun began to shine brightly making it difficult to exam his eyes. So doing next best we brought a blanket off of our bed and she worked under the blanket. Only at a mission site would this occur.

We held five days of clinic at the same setting. Most of our patients were older. With the physical exercise of walking the people do in the city, we found many patients well into their 90's. Some of the little old women from outside the city all came in a group wearing their aprons and head scarves looking quite unique in their attire. Rarely would we get a well-dressed individual in the free clinic. We instructed Alexander to only let the underserved in, and he exclaimed before we left that a lot of people are mad at him and he has to live there. He was an asset

Dr. Courtney working under a blanket

to our team and also provided a wonderful shoulder rub to a tired VOSH team member. He was my friend! Another great guy was a local optometrist, Andy. He spoke some English and had worked with us in 2008, so he assisted with the auto refractor and in the glasses distribution area on occasion.

Our meals were provided by the Rotary of Targoviste and held at a seminary school cafeteria nearby. Religion is mostly Orthodox in Targoviste. This city stands on the very edge of the Carpathian foothills and around 50 miles north of Bucharest. The population is around 90,000 and what you see are masses of concrete buildings. Many clothes drying on lines are strung outside the windows of these tall buildings.

There are some ruins dating back to 1397. In the mid-15th century Vlad Dracula added the freestanding Sunset Tower. Today it functions as a museum. A magnificent church built in 1582 stands nearby. We were able to visit this site one evening after clinic.

The Rotary was very gracious and provided our housing in a college dorm. We stayed on the second floor and held clinic in the gymnasium on the first floor. This was quite convenient. We had an entire hall of dorm rooms to choose from and kept the hall door locked as there were many other people in the building. If a team member wanted to take a little bathroom break it was easy to obtain the key and go to their second floor room. Occasionally someone would get locked in the hall and would have to wait until another team member came up with the key to get them out. If we could not find a team member in the clinic we could always go upstairs and check.

One of the characteristics of Targoviste is the multitude of stray dogs roaming the streets. There is some attempt to control this; however, I did not quite understand the program. You didn't need an alarm clock, as all dogs started to bark at the same time every day early in the morning.

During our evenings we spent time in the gymnasium socializing or playing cards. We had a pizza party one evening and another evening we joined with the Rotary for a meal and presented some gifts that we brought from the States.

Our R&R was suggested by the Rotary that we must see the monasteries of Moldavia, and they provided a bus for the trip. Our first visit was to the Bran Castle, known as Dracula's Castle that looks every inch the part. Protected by walls and pointed defense towers with few windows, we felt that indeed we were in a haunted castle. Our guide played the part and showed us hidden staircases and told the story of Dracula's visits.

We drove past haystacks that dot the scenery as we traveled into the Moldavia area. Romania is noted for its intricate gates into the yards of the homes. We saw beautiful handwork for sale along the roads. And of course the mountainous scenery was beautiful in the early fall.

Moldavia is located in eastern Romania. These beautifully painted monasteries, both inside and out containing frescoes, are in magnificent condition and were a joy to tour. We actually housed in the monastery of Petru. Thinking that we may have a rather

Drs. Gary, Bill, Jim and Albert, ODs playing cards after clinic time

barren room, I was proven wrong, as the building that we stayed in was actually quite lovely. We were served our supper meal by the monks. They brought out a full plate of polenta, a slice of onion and a large bowl of sharp shredded cheese. I thought this was to be our supper, so I piled a lot of cheese on this bland food and ate as much as I could. This plate was then taken away and another large plate with meat, potatoes and pickled vegetables was set down. By this time I was already full. We were treated very well. We visited the monastery graveyard and saw the plain wooden crosses on the graves of the sisters. Our 5 days of touring was enlightening and educational.

We finished off our mission with a few members traveling onto Istanbul, Turkey to visit the historical sites. When we travel a long distance, some members continue to enjoy Eastern Europe as an extended vacation.

We accomplished what we set out for and that is to provide free eye care to the underserved. As a team, we become lasting friends and most all members continue to sign up for other missions. It really gets you hooked. You come away with the satisfaction that you have provided some good for another person and that's what we are all about. We serve.

Perseverance

VOSH-Ohio in the Ukraine prior to the Russian Conflict 2013

It was an interesting team of 26 members, including 10 optometrists coming from many areas of the U.S., Canada and Belgium working together to provide eye care for the underserved that met in Budapest, Hungary on October 5th. Members ranged in age from 16 to 70+. The VOSH-Ohio team then traveled to Beregovo, Ukraine for their 2013 mission, the last VOSH mission into that area was in 1999. Our host was SARA, Sharing America's Resources Abroad.

We had been planning to go into Poland for a mission; however, arrangements could not be made due to elections coming up in their government. We then contacted Rev. Szilagyi, located here in Ohio, and the organization of SARA agreed to host our team.

The city of Beregovo is located in western Ukraine, near the border with Hungary. Population is around 25,000 people. This city was part of Hungary until 1919, and then became part of Czechoslovakia until 1938. It went back to Hungary from 1938 until 1944 and from that time is became part of the Ukraine. Many people in this area speak Hungarian, more so than Ukrainian. The city dates back to 1247 and has much history and interesting architecture.

Our contact for this mission was the Rev. Dr. David Pandy-Szekeres living in Hungary. David is an authorized missionary of the Presbyterian Church of Canada and is directing the Mission to

David explains some history of Beregovo to team members

ROMA Communities in Transcarpathia. He speaks fluent English, Hungarian and French and has been awarded a Diplomatic passport which affords him rapid access to border crossing and custom inspections.

David met us at the airport and transported the team to our meeting place for our late dinner. It was there we met the Szilagyi's, as they spend a few months in the Budapest area each year. We then traveled over the border into the Ukraine.

Needless to say, if rapid crossing of the border is accurate, I would not like to have a much slower crossing. Getting across the border into the Ukraine takes quite a period of time as we pass through three points of review with our passports. Once inside Ukraine, our location was nearby. We were taken to our lodging site that was a dormitory style building provided by the Hungarian Reformed Church in the area. We had a mess hall a short distance from the dorm and were provided with a bedtime snack. We were being fed very well already.

The following day we had a tour of Beregovo, seeing the deterioration of buildings not kept in repair during the communistic era. There were many monuments depicting the conflicts that had occurred in the city. The ROMA, or gypsies, strolled the pathways asking for money.

Our clinic was set up in buildings of the Reformed Church, near to the main city church. You were able to hear the massive church bells chiming during clinic time. Patients were eager for their free eye care and they crowded around the doors to our clinics, making entrance into the clinics a near impossible task. Lack of security made it quite difficult to make the patient flow go smoothly. We actually formed a chain of team members and tried to push the patients back from the door in order to get patients in and out of the building. David had not asked for security from the police and I believe this was because he had not registered this clinic with the government. He said that if he had worked through the government, we would not have been allowed to enter the country. So we worked through the masses the best we could. We found that most patients spoke Hungarian even though they reside in the Ukraine. Road signs for towns are posted in Hungarian and Ukrainian.

We held clinics in the villages of Dercen, Peterfalva and Nagydobrony. All these villages were close by; however, roads in the Ukraine are full of pot holes making travel rather slow. We held clinics two days in Beregovo and then traveled to the outlying villages for the next three days of clinics. All areas were served by the Reformed Church. A few ROMA patients were seen in our clinic. At most clinic sites where we have worked, vendors set up their food stands. It was quite different here in the Ukraine, as a vendor offered used shoes for sale outside our clinic site.

2,693 patients were cared for in our five days of clinics. Some interesting cases were cared for. A foreign body in a patient's eye was removed successfully with a business card and no anesthesia by our Belgium OD. The eye then was flooded with antibiotic

Dr. Omar and patient

solution and the patient was happy to have an eye that no longer caused him pain. Our Belgium OD, Dr. Omar, actually has a Canadian passport, has lived in Haiti and New Zealand, and is a world traveler. With his experience he was a great asset to our team.

A family came into our clinic with copies of MRI slides showing a growth behind the eye of their young son. His eye was bulging and this prompted the investigation. The family was hesitant to proceed with surgery and wanted a second opinion. We were fortunate to have a neurologist from Seattle as a team member and he was brought in to evaluate the MRI slides. His recommendation was to proceed with the surgery as no other option was available. The family accepted his opinion. We were fortunate to have Dr. Tom with the team.

Our youngest member, Phoenix, was quite a trooper. He ran the auto refractor most of the time, a task that can be quite tiring. The stamina of youth is something to be desired. We also had a few new team members that fit in quickly to our process, helping to make this a successful mission.

Everywhere we served patients some were turned away due to the large crowds and limit of daylight available in our clinics. Our team worked long hours, churches in the area provided our evening meal and travel back to our lodging place was late in the evening.

We found that most patients preferred two pair of glasses verses bifocals. Our supply of glasses provided by the Pandora Sorting Center held out rather well; however, we did have a few pairs of glasses made for patients in the Ukraine, as our inventory was not capable of providing some specific scripts.

We lodged in dorms provided by the church, sharing a coed bathroom. We developed a sign to hang on the shower door indicating if it was in use for a man or woman. This worked some of the time! As team members we become a family for this short period of time until we depart and go our separate ways.

Wonderful meals were provided by the churches. We loved the cabbage rolls, golden mashed potatoes and pork schnitzel. Pickles and tomatoes were plentiful for every meal. Patients brought candy and other gifts to the clinic to express their thanks.

After clinic on our last night we visited an orphanage for girls that was established 20 years ago by the Reformed Church. The girls were aware that our team was to visit, so they prepared a program of songs and a Hungarian dance for the team. This orphanage holds 75 to 80 girls, mostly with handicaps. A few of these girls have gone onto moving out and into marriage; however, many have not. The church is dedicating a "Care House" for the girls over 18 years of age, as they will continue to live in a protected environment for their life time. Beginning funds for this endeavor has come from an industrialist from Holland. This was a great closure for the team as we finished our mission work for the people of Ukraine in 2013.

After clinic we traveled back to Budapest and packaged a tour for the team. We had lodging in the Ecumenical Council of Churches in Hungary. We then traveled on to Bratislava, Slovakia and to

Prague, Czech Republic for a two night stay with visits to cultural sites. We stopped in Vienna, Austria to visit some sites of interest and returned again to Budapest. Tour guides were available for all cities making this an interesting and educational experience for the team.

Hope for Haiti 2015

Haiti occupies the western portion of the island of Hispaniola, while the eastern half is Dominican Republic. Its population is approximately 7.5 million, mostly descendants of slaves brought to the French colony. The language spoken is Creole, a combination of French and dialect from Africa. Haiti is the poorest country in the western hemisphere wrought with internal strife and ruled by corrupt dictators for nearly 100 years.

This is my third trip into Haiti. The first one being in 1996, I vowed then not to return. It was 92 degrees and so hot upon our arrival, we had no electricity in our compound for 3 consecutive days, only generator power for a couple of hours at the supper time, meaning no fans and sleeping on the second floor under a tin roof with breadfruit falling on the roof, was not my feeling of any comfort. We had eight women in our small dorm room, with one toilet we did not always flush, did not contribute to my liking. The story that I tell about myself is... I asked for a Band-Aid to place on my nose, as my glasses were sliding down making my nose irritated. I placed this Band-Aid on in the morning with no light in our dorm, and wore it all day until coming home in the evening, when there was some generator power to see what I looked like. Thanks to one of my fellow nurses, I had been wearing a Snoopy Band-Aid all day! I can imagine the impression I gave as I visited local doctors in their clinics and introduced myself, as the Director of Nursing of the Bluffton Hospital, with a Band-Aid on my nose.

This was a medical mission with doctors and nurses caring for children. Whatever we did would last such a short time, as worm medicine and 30 days of vitamins. I came home with the feeling of not accomplishing anything worthwhile with a long term effect.

Since that time many years ago, I have traveled on many, more missions and discomfort is minimal to the rewards that are received. I found that the distribution of glasses, to those unable to see clearly, became a longer lasting way to help people, and I have stayed with the VOSH missions over the years. I figured if I can wear my same glasses for 15 years, possibly with care others will have the same experience.

VOSH-Ohio was contacted in 2008 to develop an optometric team for Haiti. The date was set for January, 2010. The team spent a week at the SOLT mission compound and was there when the massive 7.8 earthquake struck on January 12th killing 250,000 people. This was the first eye care team to go into the SOLT mission, and over 2,500 patients were cared for at this time. Getting out of Haiti was our challenge, as refuges in a U.S. Air Force cargo plane. It was quite an experience.

VOSH-Pennsylvania requested assistance for a team to go into the northern city of Cap Haitian, Haiti in January, 2011. A VOSH-Ohio team was pulled together to provide eye care, and some of this existing team for 2015 also participated in the Cap Haitian mission.

So we were anxious to go back and see the SOLT mission compound and see the changes that had occurred in Haiti in the past 5 years ago. We received invitations to return to Haiti in January 2014, taking one year to make arrangements with our four hosts, who were involved in this current mission. Our plans were to spend three days at the SOLT mission, travel towards Port-au-Prince, stopping to care for children in an orphanage, and then continue to the Grace Children's Hospital for 2 days of clinic.

The eye care team, composed of 14 members, arrived in Port-au-Prince in the afternoon of January 10, 2015. Due to our drivers not speaking English and the team not able to communicate in Creole, we had some difficulty in knowing who was to drive the team to the compound. And also who was to help us with our luggage. This is one problem that most all visitors have in the Haiti airport, as men swarm around visitors trying to help with luggage, and then asking enormous fees for their service. Our 10 pieces of luggage got into the hands of unwanted helpers who asked for a $40 tip to pull the luggage a short distance and load them into the bus. I did pay them $30 much to my dismay and to his also.

Two of our members were not at the airport to meet up with the team. After some investigation we found that the airplanes departing from Miami had late departures. One member soon arrived and then making arrangements for the last member to be driven to the compound after the team, we took off on a three hour bus ride northward late in the afternoon and arriving in Kobonal in the province of Hinche in time for supper. The roads near Hinche were unpaved, full of bumps and chuckholes, and many people were seen to be walking on the dusty, grimy roadsides. The ever present dusty environment was later noted to be a contributing cause of the external eye disease, pterygium.

This was the same compound where we held clinic five years previously, behind a fence and protected by guards and guard dogs. We always felt safe. Father Glenn had been raising funds to care for his community when we were present before. Since the earthquake and having more mouths to feed, he has joined with the Cross Catholic organization to assist with his program. It was the Catholic organization that I had worked with to provide information and plans for the team's visit. Tent cities were built near this compound after the earthquake; however, they have been mostly replaced with permanent structures now. The unpaved roads have been paved. There is some improvement visible.

I helped to encourage an ophthalmologist to follow up with our cataract referrals from our last visit and a man from south-west Ohio was willing to travel to Haiti and see the patients. In these past years he is making a yearly trip to SOLT and has set up a clinic in the sewing room to process the surgical patients. Upon our arrival we saw two large pieces of equipment recently sent to the compound, and after viewing the clinic room it reminded me of a complete surgery suite.

During the late 8:20 p.m. dinner of rice with creole sauce, okra dish, and chicken we met and talked with Father Glenn who was in charge of this Catholic Outreach Mission, a 22 acre gated compound. He expressed his appreciation for our presence to provide eye care for the community of hundreds of the poorest of the poor. Father Glenn's mission provided education for 1,300 children, 850 children at the present site where we stayed, and the remaining children up in a mountain school. Nearly a dozen indoor-outdoor classroom buildings are within the compound.

Soon after the early mass service was completed on Sunday morning, the team set about preparing the "stations" for the clinic to see 175 men, women and children. In the course of our screening for ocular pathology, many numbers of adults were noted to suffer from mild to significant pterygium resulting from frequent exposure to sun, wind and dust. The end result would be distorted cornea with reduced visual acuity. All of this is caused by the local environment, and protective eye wear was sorely lacking for prevention of pterygium. Cataract and glaucoma, as well as pterygium cases severe enough for surgical intervention and medical management were referred, anticipating the arrival of ophthalmic surgeons in the following week.

Early awakening was no problem since the roosters would crow about 4:30 a.m. along with the bleating of the goats. Breakfast of juice, coffee, scrambled eggs was always a welcoming food to begin the day. By 7:30 a.m. many people were arriving and lining up for the clinic, many walking as far as 7 miles, and we hurriedly organized each station to begin the onslaught. To communicate with patients we were fortunate to have the help from several interpreters, some were teachers at the compound. In the course of seeing 334 people that day more pathology were seen including a case of extreme evulsion of the eye. This case was referred to the Eye Clinic at Grace Children's Hospital. This was visibly the worst case that I had ever seen, as the eye was bulging extensively.

Having finished in the late afternoon before darkness set in, the team had the opportunity to see/tour Father Glenn's farm project. Within the compound were seen chickens, guinea hens, goats and other animals. Outside the walls were vast areas of vegetables such as cabbage, okra, peppers and fruits such as plantain and melons. This was the same place the team of 2010 had been when the earthquake struck Haiti, visiting the gardens. At this time we did not feel the intense vertigo, instead a double rainbow appeared while we were in the garden. How inspiring! These fruits and

Another mode of transportation in Hinche

veggies became the mainstay of food for the school children two meals per day, and of our daily meals. Father Glenn also provides work for the 130 or so people it takes to maintain the farm gardens and the compound.

When nightfall came so did a smattering of rain which allowed the dust to settle for a day. The next morning we loaded the equipment, meds and glasses on the pickup truck. The team crammed together onto the two pickup trucks, and headed for Hinche to a Mother Theresa Sisters of Charity Hospital. The ride allowed us to witness the mode of travel noted in that region. Some young men were on motorcycles, while children and others walked, often for miles daily. Others were riding on donkeys, or donkeys loaded with goods, or people pushing wheelbarrows often seen walking barefooted.

At the hospital 128 people were screened for pathologies, anomalies and need for glasses. Done by late morning, one of the sisters gave us a tour of the facility. She came to Haiti from India, having served there under Mother Theresa, and deeply committed to rescuing the debilitated children. It touched our hearts and affected us greatly to see the babies suffering from malnutrition, the children and adults afflicted with HIV, and tuberculosis caused by a strain of HIV.

After a short lunch upon our return to the compound, we set about screening 290 children schooled there. Fortunately very few children were found to require eye care or glasses. Every student from grades one through six were noted to be dressed neatly in the uniforms, and very well behaved and organized. It was a joy to see them marching and singing as they entered the compound for classes. Monday, January 12, 2015 was the 5 year date remembering the earthquake, and all schools were closed for that day.

Day four began with a sad goodbye to Father Glenn and his staff, loading up our luggage and equipment on a bus, and away we went on the road to Port-au-Prince. Meanwhile, we made a stop in Despinos, Croix-de-Bouquet to screen the eyes of children at Imagine Mission Orphanage. The orphanage was located in a desert area north of PAP, a drab-looking environment. An optometrist from Ohio, who directs this orphanage, recommended to the VOSH-Ohio Board that they may be interested in examining the children. A request was made and fortunately we already had arrangements to visit Haiti, so seeing that it was on our travel path from Hinche to PAP, we communicated that we would be able to honor their request. Melissa, a native Ohioan, ran the orphanage with energy and enthusiasm. Members from the board living in Ohio traveled down after Christmas and had all children registered, so that when we arrived there we could easily screen the kids.

Over a 100 children lived in the orphanage, and along with other members of the community we screened 192 patients. The children were much fun to work with and so adorable. They exuded joy and laughter, perhaps oblivious to the blight and plight for life that existed beyond the walls of the orphanage. Chickkungunya had been present in this area, as all over Haiti, and some of the visitors and children had experienced this virus, which affects the joints with some long term effects. The CDC had advised people going into Haiti to wear long sleeves and long pants if possible in the heat, and use lots of DEET. It was the dry season and we were blessed not to have any problems with this disease.

The one-hour travel from Despinos to Port-au-Prince allowed us a glimpse of the market area in the city. It was not a pretty sight, for garbage and trash were strewn about with vendors selling their goods and produce in the midst of the debris, with the mass of humanity moving in every which way, and nightmarish traffic congestion. Our original plan was to visit the Iron Market located in the most inner part of PAP; however, we were discouraged to consider this move. Melissa from the orphanage had some artisans

Downtown Port-au-Prince

bring their wares to her home for us to purchase before we traveled to PAP. The Iron Market is a large place where artisans display their hand crafts. We were happy with the choices we had at the orphanage, and after driving through the turmoil of the market, we felt it was indeed unsafe to venture out of the safety of our bus. We passed demonstrators in the area and police in full military garb directing traffic. We viewed a tank with military persons as we passed through the streets. Demonstrations were supposed to be non-violent; however, at one time the news media mentioned that rocks were thrown, tires were burned and some shots were fired.

When darkness set in we arrived at Grace Children's Hospital where we unloaded all our equipment and glasses, and we viewed the location where we would hold our clinic. VOSH-Ohio had planned to visit this hospital back in 2010 to view the area and see if we could set up a clinic for a later date; however, the earthquake hit 3 days before our planned visit, the hospital was partially destroyed and our contact was killed. Final arrangements for this visit indicated that we were the first eye care team to be able to set up a clinic in this newly built facility.

Thankfully, we arrived at Wall's International Guest House just in time to enjoy a nice buffet dinner. Most of us were housed in 8 feet by 8 feet rooms with three beds to a room! Shared bathrooms were nearby. And the guest house provided a cold swimming pool to refresh your feet. Many other teams from the U.S. and Canada use this guest house as a stopping off place, as they continue on with their missions. The owner is a woman from Michigan. She inherited the guest house from her parents and visits monthly to check with the hired Haitians that run the business. During the earthquake in 2010 one building was destroyed and 5 people were killed. This has since been rebuilt and the guest house is a good reprieve in a city of poverty.

On the 5th day we arrived at Grace Children's Hospital, where hundreds of people in line awaited our presence, and we made a scramble to arrange our appropriate stations. Once we got started, it was at a blistering pace in a hot, humid environment seeing approximately 500 people, noting numbers who needed glasses and sunglasses, having ocular pathologies requiring further eye care. A short 20 minute break was had for lunch, comprised of a simple sandwich with one slice of cheese and thin meat and bottled water. At days end we were exhausted.

We met many interesting people who were helping the Haitian population. One young girl from Florence, KY moved to Haiti immediately after graduating from college. She was working in a school and absolutely loved her work and the children. She was donating one year of her life to help the children of Haiti. Others working with the children in schools and orphanages are hoping that our team could return and provide a clinic within their area.

Day six, the last day of clinic arrived, and off we went back to Grace Children's Hospital, again awaited and greeted by hundreds of people, making it difficult to ascend the outdoor stairs to our clinic area. Once we started clinic there was no stopping, except

Haitian student nurses offered to assist in the clinic

for lunch of a peanut-butter and jelly sandwich, as patients made their way from station to station. Many related that they never had their eyes checked. The chief nurse administrator couldn't thank us enough, and with tears in her eyes, told us of phone calls from people who told her how warmly and kindly they were treated. Approximately a thousand people were seen in two days. The remainder of our 4,000 pairs of glasses were left at the Grace Eye Clinic for their use.

The last visit before we went to the airport took us to a Haitian Interdenominational Shelter Home for Children run by Hal and Chris Nungester, from Ohio, who sold their possessions in stateside and came to Haiti some 12 years ago to provide for the desperate children. It was heart rendering to see the little children rush to the team members wanting to be carried, and clinging to them, crying for love and affection. Hal and Chris had 4 children and 2 adopted children from Korea before they came to Haiti. Now Hal tells us his family totals 11 with their adopted Haitian kids. Hal teaches at a Christian School and Chris works placing adoptions, and flying kids to Shriners Hospitals in the States for medical and surgical care. VOSH-Ohio also missed a visit to the orphanage back in 2010 when the earthquake damaged the Nungester's 15 foot wall around their home, decreasing it to the now 8 foot wall. The house was also damaged and for a period of time they slept out-of-doors. While the Nungester's were back in the States over Christmas, contact was made and plans developed for some of their children and teachers from the orphanage to provide assistance as interpreters for VOSH at the Grace clinic.

Haiti is a country of extreme poverty with 80% unemployment, unsanitary conditions (Port-au-Prince has a population of 3 million with no sanitary system) and little hope for its people and its children. The Ohio VOSH team has been humbled by the week's experience, but blessed for the opportunity to serve the less fortunate. For the 14 member VOSH team from Ohio, MD, and BC, Canada, it was a memorable mission, a great working team having served 2,126 people in all.

I am hoping for a return visit, as the team has invitations back to Grace Children's Hospital and a couple other sites. The children are adorable. The adults are appreciative of care. I don't know if Haiti will ever be able to care for itself. There are many NGOs

Dr. Tanner, from Canada, with children from HIS Home for Children

that return to the island and help out, then another hurricane, earthquake, flood etc. ravages the island and they start over again. The government has always been one problem, and at the present time the demonstrators want the government changed again. In 1996 the UN was present upon our arrival and in 2010 the army protected the airport when we arrived. Again in 2015 the UN was present.

Haiti, the Pearl of the Antiques, has been ravaged with tree stripping, soil erosion, fish bed disturbances and so much over the years that to overcome these obstacles is nearly impossible. Population control does not appear to exist when you see the masses walking the streets in the city and villages. To be born into this situation is distressing, as many people would like to better themselves, but have no income to make this possible. There is something about Haiti that draws you back and I am hoping to return again to this most impoverished country in our hemisphere.

The Villages of Romania 2015 with an International Team

I was contacted by an optometrist, Holly, who had been on her first VOSH-Ohio mission into Romania in 2012. She was anxious to go back into Romania and a patient of hers, Elena, had requested VOSH to provide eye care in her villages in the poorest area of northeastern Romania.

Elena was born in Romania to a large family and lived in a small, two-room, mud-walled home until her father died at an early age. She was placed into a boarding school, as her mother was unable to feed and care for herself, the grandmother and the nine children. Elena lived in a boarding house until she was old enough to care for herself. She had been brought up in a Christian home and when asked to smuggle Bibles into communistic Romania, she consented. Elena attempted to leave Romania and escape into Yugoslavia, while she was being observed by the secret police and she feared for her safety. She was later arrested and placed into prison for her attempt to leave the country. This was to be a 2 year sentence. With the assistance of Christian Aid for Romania, her prison term was reduced to 6 months. When Elena was released her citizenship was revoked and she later came to the U.S. to live. It was here that she became a patient of our Ohio optometrist.

I was able to meet Elena when I traveled to Holmes County during an ice storm in the winter of 2013. My husband didn't believe that anyone would travel in such terrible conditions, but I was determined to meet Elena and begin to discuss our upcoming mission. Our car was coated with ice when we returned home, evidence of such a violent storm. August 27 through September 10, 2015 were the dates agreed upon by Elena for the next mission into Romania for our VOSH group.

Elena now lives in Romania and travels extensively still working with Christian Aid Ministries, previously Christian Aid to Romania. She is responsible for the medicine program for CAM which helps thousands of people. With her phone service being able to call all over the world, I marveled at that fact when I received a call from Romania on my cell phone here in Bluffton, Ohio.

I visited Christian Aid Ministries headquarters, housed in Berlin, Ohio, and saw the extensive volunteer service that is provided by this organization. We were able to ship our glasses in February by cargo ship in a shipping container to a warehouse owned by the organization, and there the glasses safely remained until the team arrived in August to begin our clinics.

I began building a team and found that the timeframe chosen for this mission ran into conflicts with many of our usual team members. We were hoping to have adequate number of optometrists to provide two small teams, and travel into small villages, where it was difficult for people to obtain eye care services locally. We packed our glasses in January, not knowing if we would be able to split the large team into two smaller teams. Duplicate boxes of similar glasses scripts were numbered as team one or team two, in order for the teams to have equally a full component of glasses and instruments when they would travel to the clinic sites in the villages.

I advertised in the VOSH International website, along with the VOSH-Ohio website. I sent notices to all VOSH-Ohio members and my distribution list of optometrists that have been on previous missions.

We began to get optometrists to sign up for the mission. Holly and Jim were our husband and wife team that would be acting as the lead optometrists. Therefore, one would go with each small team to the clinic site. Another optometric husband and wife team signed up. We finally were getting enough optometrists to split into the two teams, with three ODs on each team. Even our lay members were not overly abundant. Then I received a request from an optometrist from Australia. I was thrilled! She told me during our mission that her idea of joining with a mission group was to learn how to develop her own mission.

Later on I received a request from an OD from Bucharest, Romania. We now had four ODs for each team. It was all working out for the best. I inquired to Valy, a friend from a previous Targoviste, Romania mission, and he wanted to travel over to spend a partial week with the team and would bring Andy, our OD friend from previous missions in Romania. Things were really looking good. Another request from an optometric student from the Netherlands came in. Our advertising sure paid off. What an international team we were developing.

This has been my passion to develop teams, coordinate the mission, and have happy patients in the third-world clinic sites. It was beginning to look like it would materialize. Later on I received an e-mail from our SARA friends, Sharing America's Resources Abroad, asking to join the team for a couple of days to assist with the clinics. VOSH had a team in the Ukraine with SARA as our host back in 2013 and we had met both husband and wife at that time. They were living near Budapest, Hungry for this summer and would like to drive over. I now had 22 members signed up. It was great!

I met with Elena again here in Ohio. I emailed Pastor Dan in Suceava, as he was to coordinate lodging, food, transportation, interpreters and clinic sites with patients in the area for the villages of Burdujeni, Ipotesti, Dumbraveni, Radauti, Vicov, Patrauti and

Calafindesti along with two sites in Suceava. We would lodge at the Philadelphia Christian School in Suceava with breakfast and evening meals being provided by the school.

The time finally arrived. Eight members flew out of Detroit to Cluj, Romania. We met others in either Newark or later in Cluj, as Elena indicated that getting glasses through customs was easier in Clju than trying to send them to Suceava. Christian Aid Ministries has warehouses in both Cluj and Suceava. We rented a van and were picked up at the airport. This van was with us from Friday through Sunday when we were dropped off at the Philadelphia School in Suceava.

Cluj-Napoca is the cultural and economic hub of Transylvania. In the city center, medieval town houses along with Hungarian and Habsburg buildings stand. Many museums and churches lined the streets. We were able to travel through this beautiful city and enjoy the architecture. Elena mentioned that this is the second largest city in Romania, Bucharest being the largest.

Upon our arrival, after an all-night flight, we were treated to lunch by our host and then taken to the hotel. This hotel was quite cozy situated near a lake and close to a large mall. This provided the team a place to walk, after the long airplane travel.

On Saturday we enjoyed a wonderful European breakfast at the hotel with meats, cheese, tomatoes, cereal, breads, eggs, strong coffee and much more. We traveled to a scenic area around Clju to view the area and also visited a salt mine located near Turda. The commercial operation closed down in the 1930s, but the salt mine with its bell-shaped chambers have been turned into a visitor attraction. This was quite enjoyable, as we climbed up and down steps into the depth of the mine. We then traveled to Elena's small church to examine 50 of their elderly church members in what I called a mini-clinic. Scripts were written and glasses were to be filled when we opened up the glasses container in Suceava. Elena would then bring the glasses back for the patients.

Sunday we traveled to Suceava, stopping on the way for a picnic. Sitting outdoors surrounded by the beautiful Carpathian Mountains, we enjoyed the beautiful scenery. We did have a couple of stops along the way to visit a church and castle of Dracula. Anything with the name Dracula attracts the tourists and is a very lucrative part of the Roman tourist industry.

When we arrived at the Philadelphia Christian School it was in the midst of a heat wave, as temperatures were in the 90s compared to the usual 70 degrees. Our rooms were on the top floor of the dormitory, resulting in a 60 step climb to top. For the younger team members, this was a "piece of cake". For myself I planned on climbing these stairs only once a day. So when we returned back home from clinic and after supper that is where I retired. Some team members found their way to a local watering hole to cool down after the heat of the day. They were quite accommodating and brought me back a bottle of Pepsi!!

Actually I did travel the steps twice on one day as the team went to the Detatea de Scaun Citadel, the impressive ruins of Suceava's medieval fortress as it looms above the town. Founded in 1388,

Celeste, from The Netherlands, and Dr. Lauren, from Australia enjoy a picnic

the castle has a moat and 6 foot thick walls and circular bastions. Suceava is one of the medieval capitols of Moldavia and has historic buildings and museums in the town center. Some members walked through the fort while others enjoyed a coke in the nearby café. While traveling throughout Romania you see many horse drawn wagons. With the exception of the large cities, these are a mode of travel throughout the country side and quite interesting, depending upon the type of load that is placed in the wagons.

As we form our team and assign roommates we try to assign at least two members per room. One woman from Ohio roomed with a team member from Romania. The girl from Australia roomed with the girl from the Netherlands. This makes these missions so very interesting, learning about other customs and culture around the world. Our lodging was quite adequate. We even had two bathrooms on this trip, one each for men and women. We had a small social area with comfortable seating in the hall, so that everyone could get on their internet connections, emails and Facebook. It was almost like home!

Clinics were set up mostly in the basement of churches in the villages. We took fans with us as we traveled to the clinic sites, and

Typical horse drawn wagon

it was mostly comfortable to work. Our interpreters were great. All were youth and spoke English quite well. Our transportation to the clinics was by private cars. We would start out no later than 8 am, a little later than I would have desired, and we traveled to the villages, mostly not too far away. The longest travel time was one hour. We would set up our clinic for the day in large rooms. We would scope out the best way for traffic flow and each individual in charge of their work station would start setting up clinic. By the end of the week we were all quite efficient at setting up and tearing down. Patients in mass were kept in the upper level of the church, so patient flow went smoothly. We had no mob situations. What a great way to provide services.

One of our auto refractors was not working well, so at the last minute I contacted our Romanian ODs to see if they would have an auto refractor. Helena, the OD from Bucharest, indeed had a table top auto refractor and brought it with her as she traveled by car. That was much appreciated. As she traveled back by train and unable to take the auto refractor, we worked out where the instrument was returned to Targoviste with other Romanian friends. From Targoviste the auto refractor would be sent to Bucharest. We packed it extra carefully and protected this valuable instrument as we traveled. So when our trailer came off the van with the luggage packed in it, the auto refractor was safely stored in our van. Now I'm getting ahead of my story.

Our meals consisted of mostly chicken, yellow potatoes and lots of slaw. We had cabbage rolls and vegetable soup on many occasions. All the meals were great. Our team had the privilege of having our lunch served by Elena's sister in Patrauti, which was Elena's home town. Her sister had nine children and was accustomed to serving large crowds. Elena herself married late and never had children. Elena's sister had a baby grand piano made in Vienna, Austria. Some of the interpreters played and it sounded so beautiful. I also had an opportunity to play a little. As we traveled along many flowers were seen surrounding most all homes. Roses were blooming profusely. Most homes had their own grape vines. Gates and fences surround each home. Some of the fancy wood-carved gates were seen later as we traveled on our R&R. These are mostly in the Maramures area of northern Romania, as this area is often called the land of wood and the woodcutters are widely respected for their carpentry skills, developed over the past 900 years.

Both teams cared for a total of 3,548 patients in our five days of full clinics and the mini-clinic held in Cluj. The clinics went quite smoothly, with the exception of the electricity did not meet the 220 level for use with a convertor, but was over 110, so we were unable to plug in directly. Valy, our Romanian friend, charged up our batteries from his car battery and we were in business. We were not able to use the recorder with our auto refractor, as it was not battery operated. Therefore we scribed the results of the auto refractor by hand and that was my job that I love anyway.

Working in my job I did not receive as much patient contact as I would have liked, as a volunteer our reward is to receive the thanks from the patients. That's what brings volunteers back year after year. I did on the last day of clinic climb the stairs to the sanctuary level of the church, passing through a stairway full of patients. On my way up and down men would grab my hand to kiss it. People are always so very thankful for our services. This is something I have known since our first mission; however, it was great to be reminded.

We started our R&R on Saturday when Ioana and Tony, friends from Targoviste, drove into the school's parking lot with a rented van pulling a trailer. Ioana and Tony had agreed to provide a tour package of the Maramures Region in northern Romania traveling from Suceava back to Cluj where we would board our airplane for home. The entire luggage was piled into the trailer and our 21 seat van held the remaining fourteen team members. Some members needed to return home for previous commitments and were unable to join with the R&R package offered.

We began our travels in the Bucovina Region. Bucovina is renowned for its natural beauty and for its medieval churches with gorgeous frescoes. Our first stop was in Patrauti to visit an Orthodox Church. The stone church was built by Stephen the Great in the 15th century. This is a UNESCO site, as are many of the places that we would visit. The clergy was invited to discuss the "The Holy Cross" Church and answer any questions that we may have. One of our members, Ken, must have asked him a rather controversial question and the priest's response was rather sharp. We reminded Ken to be careful with his questions from then on, as we don't to provoke an international incident.

We continued to visit monasteries of Humor built in 1530 and resembles a mini-citadel with a freestanding watchtower; Voronet with walls painted in 1540s; Sucevita was the last built of the 22 painted churches in Moldavia; and Moldovita with one of the most important murals in all of the painted churches. Each of these monasteries is painted differently with murals depicting scenes of earth and heaven. We listened to the beautiful church bells and viewed the meticulous grounds covered with roses and other flowers.

We stopped at the Black Ceramic center in Marginea and viewed a potter working at the wheel. We also stopped at a traditional workshop and Egg Museum near Moldovita with a demonstration of Painting Easter Eggs. It was thrilling to see how the various colors of paint are added to paint these intricately painted eggs. Thousands of eggs were on display throughout the shop.

Our lodging was in pensions. These are houses that offer breakfast and evening meal with the lodging. On our first stop in Vama, team members were in two near-by houses, with the meal being served in the main house. Wonderful meals were served and hosts of the pensions offered the traditional plum brandy, the national drink, to our members.

We had an excursion on a Mocanita Train pulled by an old steam engine. This was about an hour's trip through the countryside and enjoyed by all members. Hearing the whistle blow as we bounced along at a very slow speed was refreshing. We passed by homes painted with designs and flowers and farms with the traditional hay stacks. Animals were viewed along the way. And the most interesting part was the group of native history buffs following the train from the starting point, climbing in cars to follow the train, and arriving at the departure point. They were taking photos of the whole process and we were taking photos of them, taking photos of us. The van caught up with the team on departing the train and we continued on our tour.

Driving through the Carpathian Mountains we would pass trucks filled with logs. All mountains in Romania are the Carpathian, whether they are the Southern Carpathian, Northern Carpathian or Eastern Carpathians. Roads were narrow, twisting and turning as we traveled. Our visit to a local farm was very interesting. The farmer had one cow, two pigs and a few chickens. He raised rows and rows of cabbage and had multiple large wooden barrels over eight feet high and quite large in diameter where he soaked either pickles or cabbage in salt water. Pickles were soaked for a short time and then canned as dill pickles. The cabbage was soaked for months as a whole head and then was sold as pickled cabbage to be used to make cabbage rolls. We were greeted with the typical Romanian brew and we were able to taste the pickles, cabbage and also a pork sausage roll, all made from farm produce. This type of farming appeared to help the farmer financially, as he had built a new house beside the older traditional house and had a Mercedes sitting in the driveway.

We were able to stop at a local market in Bodgan Voda. There was used clothing available for sale, fresh vegetables that looked wonderful, and animals. It had rained before our visit, so we walked carefully through the mud and animal droppings. Food was being cooked outdoors and for sale to those wanting to take the risk. Many farmers brought their smaller animals in by horse and wagon. We met a woman that wanted to sell her pig. Our tour director told her that Ken, one of our team members, had 1,300 pigs at home and she answered by saying…"Does he want to buy one more?" You can see why we are called Rich Americans. It fascinates me that all women and girls in the country wear head scarves to the market, to church and elsewhere. Perhaps that is what I should have invested in. Due to my thinning hair, I found it difficult to maintain a decent appearance, so I opted on wearing a ball cap the entire mission. Along with my roommate who wore a wig, we fit in quite well together. It didn't take us long to do our hair each morning. My roommate slept in bed with her wig, available at all times. At least I didn't sleep in bed with my ball cap!

We traveled on to the Maramures area. Maramures is a living embodiment of medieval Europe. It is a place where ancient traditions still remain. Maramures is often called the land of wood, as it is rich in oak and fir forests. In the Maramures Region we visited a town home and marveled at the industrious life style of this couple. Their home and out buildings were located near a stream. They had a traditional water-powered, fan-shaped wooden whirlpool for washing and fulling textiles. They had a distillery and made plum and pear brandy. Both are for the villagers' communal use. They used the water wheel to grind flour for sale. They had wool processing equipment to spin cotton for thread to make cloth items. This was in the village of Sacel. They were quite an ingenious and enjoyable couple.

And you will never know what happened next. We had traveled over the Prislop Pass as the highest elevation in the mountains and were now on straight roads when our trailer came loose from the van and veered into the ditch flying close by a woman walking in the road. What a shock and what a blessing that it didn't go over a mountain where we just traveled, and it was upright, and it did not hit the woman in the road. The team continued on to lunch, while some of the men flagged down a local priest and asked for assistance to travel to a nearby town. A bolt that had become severed caused the trailer to become disconnected from the van. The priest gladly helped the members and when the remaining team had finished their lunch at a local guesthouse in Barsana, the entire team traveled on.

Our evening in another pension in Hoteni was very interesting. This area is famous for its open-air folk music festival. So we were honored when a local musician came to provide traditional music for the team using all sorts of string instruments. He also would begin to sing quite loudly and also quite unexpectedly. This almost led to one of our members falling off her chair. It was great for a good laugh. Good food and much brandy were showered upon the group. The décor of the rooms in the houses was very interesting as brightly colored material was placed on the walls, there were many typical artifacts throughout the house. It began to become cooler and heavy blankets were needed for warmth that night.

Our next stop was at the woodcutter's home in Breb Village. The old ways still hold here. Hay stacks were plentiful throughout the fields, as cutting hay with scythes is still practiced.

Churches are constructed of wood. Picturesque timber farmhouses are seen. We visit the woodcutter's place of work we found this very interesting, as this wood cutter have sent his carvings around the world, including the U.S.A. People that are more affluent in certain areas of Romania have elaborate wood carved gates as you enter their property. Many of these gates were seen in this area of travel. We visited a wooden church in Budesti. Budesti is named after a 14th century landowner called Bud and is one of the largest villages in the Maramures. Traveling along we pass many long-haired sheep under their shepherd's care.

A fun stop was in Sarbi as we visited a hat maker. Men in a couple of local villages wear a funny little straw hat and this was the town where these hats are made. Of course, all the men in our traveling group had to get their photo taken with a little hat on their head. Sarbi has rows of the handsome carved gates. The gates are designed with rope patterns of rosettes and stick figures representing the Neolithic people who inhabited the Maramures region 7,000 years ago.

The last place of interest was the Happy Cemetery in Sapanta. This was a popular tourist stop as many tour busses pulled into the village. This cemetery had wooden crosses for markers that were painted bright colors and carry witty verses that make light of death. The markers give information about the person, along with a carved photo. The cemetery surrounded a large church that was currently under renovation.

The team stopped at a hat maker shop

We had lunch in Sighetu Marmatiei, a fast-growing town and known as Maramures's historic capital. We were close to the Ukraine border and could view the Ukrainian villages as we traveled along. We continued on to Cluj and our last evening together as a team, before our departure the following day to our own homes. A great mission, new friends from around the world and many, many happy patients.

Mission aborted due to a Foreign Pathogen in my Blood put me into Shock!

Nine days before departing for Haiti with an optometrist from VOSH on January 20, 2016 my desire to return to Haiti again was cancelled. Mission Possible was taking teams into their compound in Lanzac, Haiti and asked for eye care for the children in the six schools that were sponsored by the mission. Dr. Tom and I had packed glasses and instruments for the trip and were anxiously awaiting the time at 3 a.m. on the 20th when we would depart with the group of 22 members for Haiti. It had been twenty years since I first visited the mission compound and I was interested in returning. On January 11th, my birthday, I was admitted to the local hospital in septic shock. Believe me that was a shock!

It was determined the bacteremia secondary to an organism called *aeromonas sobria* was the culprit. What an experience with 10 days of hospitalization, mostly in the intensive care unit. After study it was determined that I was immunosuppressed, which probably precipitated the incident, and that this little pathogen had been harboring in my gut since some traveler's diarrhea from a previous stint out of the country. Mortality rate for the bacteria is 39%. Thank goodness I was in the 61%!

Even though we all try to be very careful when traveling, drinking bottled water and eating cooked food according to recommendations by the CDC, invariably someone comes down with the dreaded diarrhea. In fact many of the team experienced this in Romania last fall. I do not know when or where I hosted the pathogen; however, I hope it is gone by now. A visit to the Infectious Disease doctor enlightened me as to his thoughts about this rare condition. He reflected that we all carry 3 pounds of bacteria in our guts. My problem was the foreign one that I obtained. In fact I am a rare patient being investigated with a case study.

I now have plans to continue my passion only with coordinating the missions. Our next mission is scheduled for January of 2017 returning to Honduras. Boliver, who hosted our team in 2012, is happy to have a team return to the villages near Cedros. I am looking forward to working with him and knowing that my commitment for service continues, even if I have to look at photos afterwards and listen to the wonderful stories that the team shares. Knowing that volunteerism and service continue through others gives me the reward of fulfilling my passion. I will also be working on a return mission to Patzquaro, Mexico, working with the same host as in 2009. She did a wonderful job in coordinating that mission and I am looking forward to another great mission in Mexico for the team.

The need is great. The fulfillment is rewarding. The workers are few. So I challenge YOU to take the step to become involved. And don't limit your boundaries, if at all possible. It is a big world out there and so many opportunities to serve your fellow man. All it takes is perseverance!

Glossary

AIDS . . ..Acquired Immune Deficiency Syndrome

AMMID.. .. ...Association Maya-Mam Investigation and Development

ATM.. .. ..Automatic teller machine

BC, CANDA . . British Columbia

CAM . .. .Christian Aid Ministries

CDC.. .. ..Center of Disease Control

CEO .. ..Chief Executive Officer

CIA. .. ..Central Intelligence Agency

CNN.. .. ..Cable news network

CPR .. ..Cardio-pulmonary Resuscitation

DAR.. .. ..Dar es Salaam

DEET .. ..Active ingredient in insect repellent

ED .. ..Emergency department

EKG .. ..Electrocardiogram

ENT .. ..Ears, nose and throat

H1N1 .. ..Swine flu

HCFA .. ..Health Care Finance Administration

HIV .. ..Human Immunodeficiency virus in AIDS

INTEVEP .. .. .technological division of PDVSA

ISOH. .. ..International Services of Hope

JCAHO. .. .. .. .Joint commission on accreditation of Healthcare Organizations

JKF. .. .. .John F. Kennedy airport

LPN .. .. .Licensed practical nurse

MD. .. .. .Medical doctor

MRI .. .. .Magnetic Resonance Imaging

NGO.. .. .. .. .Non-governmental organizations

OD.. .. .. .Doctor of Optometry

PAP .. .. .Port au Prince

PDVSA. .. .. .. .Petroleum Division Venezuela South America

PET .. .. .Personal energy transportation

R&R.. .. .. .. .Rest and Relaxation

RN.. .. .. .Registered Nurse

ROMA .. .. .. .Gypsies

SARA .. .. .Sharing America's Resources Abroad

SOLT. .. .. .The Society of Our Lady of the Most Holy Trinity

TV.. .. .. .Television

UN.. .. .. .United Nations

UNESCO. .. .. .The United Nations Educational, Scientific and Cultural Organization

US .. .. .United States

USA .. .. .United States of America

VOSH .. .. .. .Volunteer Optometric Services to Humanity

VOSHER. .. .. .made up word! A true VOSH team member

WW II.. .. .. .. .World War Two

Volunteers serving on missions

1994 Honduras mission into Santa Barbara...

Kathy Campbell	Marlo Campbell	William Campbell, OD
John Conrad, OD	Howard Coy	Theodore Cunningham
Dorothy German, RN	Darrell Groman, OD	Morris Groman
Cindy Johnson, OD	Robert Merriam	Shirley Merriam
Zygmunt Miller	Arliss Plaugher	Barbara Plaugher, RN
Charles Risser	Louis Risser	Margaret Risser

1996 Honduras mission into Santa Barbara...

William Campbell, OD	John Conrad, OD	Howard Coy
Darrell Groman, OD	Morris Groman	Robert Merriam
Shirley Merriam	Zygmunt Miller	Arliss Plaugher
Barbara Plaugher, RN	Charles Risser	Brian Dittenber, OD
Suzie Dittenber	John Dudek	Larry Hookway, OD
Walter Jablonski		

1997 El Salvador mission into Sushitoto...

Marlo Campbell	William Campbell, OD	Howard Coy
Alice Davis, RN	John Dudek	Carol Groman
Darrell Groman, OD	Irina Groman	Morris Groman
Larry Hookway, OD	Samantha Hookway	Walter Jablonski
Zygmunt Miller	Ed Mitchell	Sharon Mitchell
Jeremy Pifer	Mark Pifer, OD	Arliss Plaugher
Barbara Plaugher, RN	Chuck Risser	

2000 Nicaragua into Esteli...

Jonathan Baumgartner	Steve Belanger, OD	Bill Campbell, OD
Howard Coy	John Dudek	Carol Groman
Morris Groman	Albert Hoffman, OD	Phil Huffman, OD
Walter Jablonski	Frank Igielski	Robin LaValley, OD
Ed Mitchell	Sharon Mitchell	Arliss Plaugher
Barbara Plaugher, RN	Carolyn Stang, Pharm D	Dick Stang, OD
Mary Elizabeth Stang, RN		

2001 Venezuela into Los Teques...

Steve Belanger, OD	Bill Campbell, OD	Marlo Campbell
Howard Coy	John Dudek	Carol Groman
Morris Groman	Alex Hookway	Amy Hookway
Larry Hookway, OD	Frank Igielski	Walter Jablonski
Ed Mitchell	Sharon Mitchell	Kevin Pifer
Mark Pifer, OD	Arliss Plaugher	Barbara Plaugher, RN
Darlene Pohlman	Jim Pohlman	Alex Pulido
Edgar Pulido	Julie Pulido	Chuck Risser
Carolyn Stang, Pharm D	Dick Stang, OD	Mary Elizabeth Stang, RN

2002 Poland into Kwdizyn...

Bill Campbell, OD	Marlo Campbell	Howard Coy
Susan Daris, OD	Jean Dudek	John Dudek
Carol Groman	Morris Groman	Frank Igielski
Walter Jablonski	Bryan Kemper, OD	Andrew McLaughlin
Arliss Plaugher	Barbara Plaugher, RN	Darlene Pohlman
Jim Pohlman	Duane Polzien	Chuck Risser
Carolyn Stang, Pharm D	Dick Stang, OD	Mary Elizabeth Stang, RN
James Winnick, OD		

2003 Honduras into Juticalpa and Tegucigalpa...

Howard Coy	Carol Groman	Morris Groman
Albert Hoffman, OD	Alex Hookway	Amy Hookway
Larry Hookway, OD	Jacob Kaufman	Robin LaValley, OD
Ed Mitchell	Sharon Mitchell	Daniel Pifer
Mark Pifer, OD	Arliss Plaugher	Barbara Plaugher, RN
Darlene Pohlman	Jim Pohlman	Chuck Risser
Carolyn Stang, Pharm D	Dick Stang, OD	Helen Zerkle

2005 Tanzania into Dar es Salaam...

Bill Campbell, OD
Lou Cyburt
Jeffrey Forrey, OD
Albert Hoffman, OD
Samantha Hookway
Frank Igielski
Tim Kraus
Philip Paros, OD
Darlene Pohlman
Tom Rippner, OD
Mary Elizabeth Stang, RN
Edwin Winbigler, OD

Marlo Campbell
Susan Daris, OD
Karl Gingrich
Amy Hookway
Don Hostetler, DVM
Walter Jablonski
Michele Lee
Mark Pifer, OD
Jim Pohlman
Carolyn Stang, Pharm D
Betty Vo, OD
Janice Winbigler

Wayne Collier, OD
John Daris
Mary Hedberg
Larry Hookway, OD
Philip Huffman, OD
Brenda Kraus, Optician
Bob Palozei, OD
Barbara Plaugher, RN
Sharon Anderson
Dick Stang, OD
Ford Warren

2006 Ecuador into El Florin...

Bill Campbell, OD
John Daris
Albert Hoffman, OD
Larry Hookway, OD
John McCarter
Arliss Plaugher
Jim Pohlman
Carolyn Stang, Pharm D

Marlo Campbell
Christina Fox, OD
Sarah Hoffman
Don Hostetler, DVM
Willene Pifer
Barbara Plaugher, RN
Joyce Ramsue-Singleton, OD
Edwin Winbigler, OD

Susan Daris, OD
Roger Heckman
Amy Hookway
Philip Huffman, OD
Mark Pifer, OD
Darlene Pohlman
Karen Saprano
Janice Winbigler

2007 Guatemala into Comitancillo...

Bill Campbell, OD
Courtney Dietzel
Albert Hoffman, OD
Brenda Kraus, Optician
Ashley Pifer
Arliss Plaugher
Jim Pohlman
Mary Elizabeth Stang, RN

Marlo Campbell
Christina Fox, OD
Amy Hookway
Ron Meyers
Willene Pifer
Barbara Plaugher, RN
Carolyn Stang, Pharm D
Edwin Winbigler, OD

Lou Cyburt
Morris Groman
Larry Hookway, OD
John Moats, MD
Mark Pifer, OD
Darlene Pohlman
Dick Stang, OD
Janice Winbigler

2008 Romania into Targoviste...

Bill Campbell, OD
Greg Hagedorn, OD
Don Hostetler, DVM
Cathy Pifer
Barbara Plaugher, RN
Dick Rumpff
Marsha Sullivan
Edwin Winbigler, OD

Marlo Campbell
Nancy Heckman
Joyce Hostetler
Mark Pifer, OD
Darlene Pohlman
Janice Rumpff, Optician
Carolyn Stang, Pharm D
Janice Winbigler

Christina Fox, OD
Roger Heckman
Amber McIntosh, OD
Arliss Plaugher
Jim Pohlman
Khadija Shahid, OD
Jane Stang

2009 Mexico into Patzquaro...

Gary Barnard, OD
Lou Cyburt
Don Hostetler, DVM
Barbara Plaugher, RN
Edwin Winbigler, OD

Bill Campbell, OD
Jerry Ferrell, OD
Walter Jablonski
Darlene Pohlman
Janice Winbigler

Marlo Campbell
Albert Hoffman, OD
Arliss Plaugher
Jim Pohlman

2010 Haiti into Hinche...

Bill Campbell, OD
Joanne Moats, RN
Arliss Plaugher
Jim Pohlman
Joyce Ramsue-Thompson, OD
Janice Winbigler

Christina Fox, OD
John Moats, MD
Barbara Plaugher, RN
Khadija Shahid, OD
Larry Swords

Ron Meyers
Mark Pifer, OD
Darlene Pohlman
Carolyn Stang, Pharm D
Edwin Winbigler, OD

2011 Peru into Iquitos...

Gary Barnard, OD
Lou Cyburt
Roger Heckman
Larry Hookway, OD
Don Hostetler, DVM
John Moats, MD
Mark Pifer, OD
Darlene Pohlman
Jane Stang

Bill Campbell, OD
Roy Ebihara, OD
Albert Hoffman, OD
Carol Huffman
Walter Jablonski
Philip Paros, OD
Arliss Plaugher
Jim Pohlman
Edwin Winbigler, OD

Marlo Campbell
Jerry Ferrell, OD
Any Hookway
Philip Huffman, OD
Ron Meyers
Cathy Pifer
Barbara Plaugher, RN
Carolyn Stang, Pharm D
Janice Winbigler

2012 Honduras into Cedros and Tegucigalpa...

Gary Barnard, OD
Brenda Kraus, Optician
Ron Meyers
Mark Pifer, OD
Darlene Pohlman
Cassandra Smith
Janice Winbigler

Christina Fox, OD
Tim Kraus
Jeanette Lam, OD
Arliss Plaugher
Jim Pohlman
Dr. Ben Szirth

Roy Ebihara, OD
Don Hostetler, DVM
Marcia Uhl
Barbara Plaugher, RN
Khadija Shahid, OD
Edwin Winbigler, OD

2012 Romania into Targoviste...

Bill Campbell, OD
Jim Conway, OD
Albert Hoffman, OD
Joanne Moats, RN
Nancy Oberholtzer
Darlene Pohlman
Meridith Walton, OD

Marlo Campbell
Courtney Dewey, OD
Donna Meyers
John Moats, MD
Arliss Plaugher
Jim Pohlman
Gary Watts, OD

Holly Conway, OD
Linda Hill
Ron Meyers
Kenneth Oberholtzer
Barbara Plaugher, RN
Janice Rumpff, Optician

2013 Ukraine into Beregovo...

Gary Barnard, OD
Judy Clifft
Joe Crosby, OD
Tom Kushner, MD
Donna Meyers
John Moats, MD
Barbara Plaugher, RN
Mark Pifer, OD
Pamela Winston, Optician

Bill Campbell, OD
Natalie Cepynsky, OD
Bob Goulding, OD
Miranda Lee, OD
Ron Meyers
Philip Paros, OD
Darlene Pohlman
Janice Rumpff, Optician
Phoenix Winston-Levesque

Marlo Campbell
Lora Cretella
Albert Hoffman, OD
Omar Lenfesty, OD
Joanne Moats, RN
Arliss Plaugher
Jim Pohlman
Barbara Talan

2015 Haiti into Hinche and Port-au-Prince...

Gary Barnard, OD
Christina Fox, OD
Micah Kraus
Joanne Moats, RN
Barbara Plaugher, RN

Roy Ebihara, OD
Ernie Hollenbacher
Jeanette Lam, OD
John Moats, MD
Tanner Udenberg, OD

Lindsay Florkay, OD
Brenda Kraus, Optician
Ron Meyers
Mark Pifer, OD

2015 Romania into Suceava...

Andrei Constantin, OD   Holly Conway, OD   Jim Conway, OD

Thomas Doyle, OD   Celeste Elizen   Lauren Jalkh, OD

John Moats, MD   Kenneth Oberholtzer   Nancy Oberholtzer

Barbara Plaugher, RN   Helena Raicu, OD   Daniel Ritter

Janice Rumpff, Optician   Eleanor Runyan   Valentin Stefan

Marius Vidikan, OD   Michelle Vidikan, OD   Drusilla Weatherby, OD

Joseph Weatherby III

References:

VOSH History. . . . . Vistakon, Division of Johnson & Johnson Vision Care, Inc.

Honduras Bay Islands Guide. . . . . J.P. Panet with Hart/Glassman

Central America - On the Loose, On the Cheap, Off the Beaten Path
. . . . Berkeley Guides

Mexico Insight Guide. . . . . Discovery Channel APA Publications

Ecuador including the Galapagos Islands .. LG Let's Go St. Martin's Press New York

Tanzania Globetrotter . . . . Graham Mercer

Poland Eyewitness Travel Guides. . . . . Dorling Kindersley Publishing, Inc.

Romania. . . . . National Geographic Traveler

Peru Eyewitness Travel. . . . . Dorling Kindersley Publishing, Inc.

Eastern & Central Europe Eyewitness Travel. .. Dorling Kindersley Publishing, Inc.

Internet articles